In the mood for
HEALTHY
FOOD

Jo Pratt

NOURISH
EAT WELL, LIVE WELL

Acknowledgements

A big healthy thank you to everyone who helped create this book…

My wonderful family and friends who have been my chief tasters, giving me invaluable inspiration and ideas along the way. At least with this book it was always healthy food – so you can't blame me for expanding waistlines this time!

A special thanks to my brilliant husband Phil and my two adorable (most of the time!) children Olly and Rosa.

Everyone at Nourish and Watkins Media, especially Grace Cheetham, for always having such enthusiasm for the book. Becci Woods and Elinor Brett for editing and fine tuning, Vicky Hartley, Francesca Yarde-Buller, Sian Jones and all in marketing, publicity and sales for shouting about the book and getting it into people's homes. Georgina Hewitt for designing and art directing, Tamin Jones for his beautiful photography, Luis Peral for creative styling, Stephanie Howard, Ellie Jarvis and Katie Marshall for assisting on the shoot. What a great team – everything looks amazing, it was such fun and a really refreshing change to tuck into a nice healthy lunch each day!

Thanks to Borra Garson and the team at DML for your continued support and making things happen.

And last but by all means not least, thank you to everyone who buys this book. I hope you enjoy using it as much as I've enjoyed putting it together.

In the mood for
HEALTHY FOOD

Jo Pratt is an acclaimed food stylist, writer and presenter. As well as being the bestselling author of five cookbooks, including *In the Mood for Food* and *The Madhouse Cookbook*, you'll also find Jo presenting recipes online, on TV and in your favourite food magazines.

Dedication
Millie, this one's for you! xxx

In the Mood for Healthy Food
Jo Pratt

First published in the UK and USA in 2015 by
Nourish, an imprint of Watkins Media Limited
19 Cecil Court
London WC2N 4EZ

enquiries@nourishbooks.com

Copyright © Watkins Media Limited 2015
Text and recipe copyright © Jo Pratt 2015
Photography copyright © Watkins Media Limited 2015

The right of Jo Pratt to be identified as the Author
of this text has been asserted in accordance with the
Copyright, Designs and Patents Act of 1988.

Publisher: Grace Cheetham
Editor: Rebecca Woods
Art Direction & Design: Georgina Hewitt
Production: Uzma Taj
Commissioned photography: Tamin Jones
Food Stylist: Jo Pratt
Props Stylist: Luis Peral

A CIP record for this book is available from the
British Library

ISBN: 978184899277-1

10 9 8 7 6 5 4 3 2 1

Typeset in MrsEaves
Colour reproduction by XY Digital
Printed in China

Publisher's note:
While every care has been taken in compiling the
recipes for this book, Watkins Media Limited, or any
other persons who have been involved in working on
this publication, cannot accept responsibility for any
errors or omissions, inadvertent or not, that may be
found in the recipes or text, nor for any problems that
may arise as a result of preparing one of these recipes.
If you are pregnant or breastfeeding or have any
special dietary requirements or medical conditions,
it is advisable to consult a medical professional before
following any of the recipes contained in this book.

Notes:
Unless otherwise stated:
· Use medium fruit and vegetables
· Use fresh ingredients, including herbs and spices
· Do not mix imperial and metric measurements
· 1 teaspoon = 5ml/^{1}/8fl oz   1 tablespoon = 15ml/^{1}/2fl oz
  1 cup = 240ml/8fl oz

nourishbooks.com

Contents

Introduction

This cookbook is all about well-balanced, fabulous-tasting recipes that will make you feel full of vitality and not full of guilt. Whatever the time of day, or day of the week, there are recipes and ideas that will satisfy your mood for food that is good for you.

It's very apparent that we are now far more conscious of what food we eat and our wellbeing than ever before. Demand for the more healthy things in life has grown massively — just check out your local supermarket or grocery stores and see the vast range of healthy ingredients from all over the world. Who knew what quinoa or flaxseed was a few years ago, except maybe that quirky art teacher who taught you at college?!

It's important to say that this cookbook isn't a diet book. There's no calorie counting, eliminating, restricting, portion controlling, fasting, detoxing — there are no rules and don't worry about this book being just a fad and ending up on a shelf in a second-hand bookshop. It'll be a book that takes pride of place in your kitchen and something you turn to for your everyday cooking and entertaining. It makes use of the wonderful ingredients you can buy and really will make a difference to how you feel about yourself.

I have put together all of the recipes so that they taste as delicious as you'd expect from a cookbook. I've then really thought about the ingredients and replaced some with more healthy alternatives — for example, how do Beef and Quinoa Meatballs sound? By reducing the meat, I've reduced the saturated fat content and really increased the overall nutrient content of the dish with the addition of quinoa.

Here's another — Kale Pesto Pasta with Crispy Prosciutto. Using kale as an alternative to basil provides a powerful boost of vitamins and antioxidants and tastes just as, if not more, delicious than regular pesto and makes you feel superhuman!

When it comes to sweet things, there is still no missing out. Try the Pear, Pecan and Spelt Cookies that don't actually contain any sugar, but still taste out of this world.

I have also added wonderfully healthy ingredients, such as chia seeds, into the recipes. Chia seeds contain everything, including vitamins A, C and D, magnesium and zinc, and are the highest known whole-food source of omega-3 fatty acids ever. Plus, they're readily available from everyday shops. I love them in my Chia Seed Flapjack recipe and as a crunchy topping for Seeded Baked Salmon with Crushed Minty Peas, making the fish double healthy.

When it comes to the actual cooking, I've also tried to be clever there, too. The recipes suggest poaching, grilling and steaming to name a few. If there is a way to make it slightly healthier without compromising on taste I've done it.

As you go through the book you'll see that I've divided it into the chapters Breakfast & Brunch, Light Meals, Main Meals and Something Sweet.

Chapter one:

breakfast & brunch

How do Buckwheat and Coconut Crêpes with Baked Figs sound? Buckwheat is high in fibre, gluten-free and contains calcium, protein, iron and B vitamins. Definitely worth getting out of bed for and will have you skipping out of the front door to tackle the day. Or, my husband's favourite breakfast EVER! Poached Eggs, Tahini and Pan-fried Avocado. It's a great hangover brunch – probably due to the protein-rich tahini and eggs. You'll also find some great drinks, amazing alternatives to high-sugar boxes of bought cereals and some sugar-free muffins.

Chapter two:

light meals

These ideas are perfect for lunches or first courses if you are entertaining. The Baked Root Vegetable Falafel with Green Yogurt always go down a storm when I serve them at dinner parties – in fact, I always make twice the amount so I've plenty for lunch the next day. I love the Fried Sesame Tofu with Soba Noodle Salad for a Saturday lunch. The tofu acts as a sponge and soaks up all sorts of lovely flavours and it's super-good for you. There are soups both light and hearty, salads for warm weather and comforting dishes for times when you need... comforting.

Chapter three:

main meals

The main meals are for the evenings, dinner parties and those lovely long weekend lunches when all your friends or family come round for a catch-up while the kids trash the place. You'll find Chicken and Date Tagine with Cauliflower 'Couscous' and Spelt and Hemp Pizzas. There are dishes that can be prepped ahead and recipes that you can throw together in no time at all, just in case you have guests drop by as a surprise.

Chapter four:

something sweet

No book of mine will ever be without desserts – so writing this chapter has been a challenge to say the least. I swapped sugar for natural sources of sweetness such as agave syrup, pure maple syrup, honey and dried fruits. I've used different flours, kept fat contents low, added courgette to a cake to give you one of your five a day and even added a couple of chocolate recipes to satisfy the chocoholics out there.

So, in a healthy Brazil nut shell, the recipes are well-balanced, nutritious, delicious, easy to shop for and cook and will help you feel less guilty next time you see a runner and feel bad you have not done any exercise for a week or so, or given in to that bag of crisps that's been calling you from inside the pantry. I'm 100 per cent positive you'll find something to satisfy all those times when you're in the mood for being healthy.

Enjoy.

Well Stocked...

Here's a list of everyday foods that I like to keep stocked up on. I find it handy to know they are there to use, as and when I require them. Otherwise I rummage around my kitchen and end up making something that isn't necessarily as healthy as I had intended. I also find that keeping the cupboard well stocked makes creating some recipes easier on the pocket, as I don't have to buy all the ingredients in one go.

You'll find as you go through this book that you use some ingredients, such as nuts, grains and spices, more than others. These ingredients are worth buying in larger quantities as it can work out to be far more cost-effective – providing you have the space to store them. I must admit that I have been known to use the top shelf of my wardrobe for dry food storage in the past!

I've put a list together of core ingredients, both fresh and dried, that not only feature quite a lot in this book, but also are very useful to have for a healthier way of living and eating.

Fresh seasonal fruits　　Try and use them when they are at their best. The exception is bananas, which make a great natural sweetener when overripe – the riper they are, the sweeter they become. Most berries can be frozen and used throughout the winter months, and are ideal for using in smoothies and baking. Included here as fruits are avocados and tomatoes (leave to ripen in your fruit bowl if they are not ripe when bought).

Fresh seasonal vegetables　　Include plenty of greens, such as kale, spinach and cabbage, broccoli, beans, roots and salads. I highly recommend you get a regular veg box delivery, which will provide you with the very best seasonal produce.

Garlic, ginger, onions　　Yes, these are a veg but worth mentioning separately as they are the perfect starting base for many savoury recipes, and ginger is great for sweet dishes, too. If you have an excess of ginger, it can be stored in the freezer.

Fresh herbs　　If you're not able grow your own in your garden or on a windowsill, then pots of growing herbs are a handy thing to have in the kitchen. They can really lift a dish with their differing flavours, not to mention provide added goodness. If you buy bags of cut herbs, a handy tip is to put them in a sealable freezer bag/sandwich bag with a splash of water and store in the refrigerator. They last far longer than if kept in the bags they are sold in.

Dried fruits	Great to use for naturally sweetening recipes, in baking and as snacks.
Wholemeal/whole-wheat and/or spelt flour	Convenient for reducing the processed wheat content of your cooking and increasing fibre.
Pure maple syrup, agave syrup and honey	All are versatile natural sweeteners and far healthier than refined sugars.
Mixed seeds	Including chia, flaxseed, pumpkin, sunflower, hemp and sesame. These are powerhouses of nutrients and extremely versatile in all types of cooking and baking.
Mixed nuts	Great for snacking on, but they also make a brilliant base for many baking recipes, plus you can even make butter and milk with them.
Coconut oil	An amazing healthy substitute for butter in all types of cooking and baking (and it is believed to have numerous beauty benefits, too).
Rapeseed/canola oil, avocado oil, olive and extra-virgin olive oil	For dressings, drizzling and cooking. Far better for you than vegetable and sunflower oil.
Mixed grains and pulses	Including quinoa, oats, pearl barley and lentils (Puy and red). Amazing as the backbone of numerous dishes, providing stacks of nutrition.
Whole-wheat pasta, rice and couscous	Much more nutritious than their white cousins.
Canned pulses	Including chickpeas, cannellini beans, butter/lima beans and kidney beans. Far more convenient than having to presoak and cook from scratch.
Firm silken tofu	A great high-protein, low-fat, long-life product to have in your cupboard for adding to broths, desserts, smoothies and pancakes.
Miso paste	For instant soup, marinades and dressings.
Dried herbs and spices	The icing on the cake for many recipes. I'd be lost without ground cinnamon, ground cumin, ground coriander, dried chilli/hot pepper flakes and oregano.
Plain yogurt	A valuable ingredient to keep in the refrigerator for breakfast, dressings, marinades, dips, sauces, desserts and baking.
Eggs	One of the most versatile and beneficial ingredients from breakfast right through to dinner.

breakfast & brunch

pineapple, mango and coconut juice

½ ripe pineapple, about
  300g/10½oz flesh,
  peeled and cut into
  chunks
1 ripe mango, peeled,
  pitted and chopped
500ml/17fl oz/2 cups
  coconut water, chilled
1 tsp grated root ginger
juice of ½ lime
ice cubes, to serve
  (optional)

The energy-giving fruit and super-hydrating coconut water in this refreshing juice drink will make you feel full of get-up-and-go: I make this most Monday mornings. The enzymes from the pineapple are great for your digestion. They maximize the extraction of all the other nutrients in the drink and will give a huge boost to your energy levels. If you are feeling really, really tired, throw a peeled banana into the blender, too, as this will provide you with a long-lasting boost of energy.

Put all the ingredients in a blender and blitz for about 1 minute until completely smooth.

Pour into glasses and serve over ice, if using, or straight.

⁎ WASTE NOT, WANT NOT

Not only is coconut water a great ingredient to use
in juices and smoothies, but you can also use it to cook rice.
It gives it a subtle flavour that works brilliantly with
a number of cuisines from around the world, such as Asian,
Indian, Caribbean or South American, to name a few.
If you have some left over after making this recipe,
why not give it a try?

blackberry and goji smoothie

4 tbsp goji berries
200g/7oz/1½ cups fresh
   or defrosted frozen
   blackberries
2 ripe bananas, peeled
   and roughly chopped
250ml/9fl oz/1 cup
   almond milk, chilled,
   plus extra if needed

I have a confession – I don't really like goji berries. I find them a little hard and chewy. However, I know they are one of the most powerful superfoods, packed with antioxidants that'll keep me looking youthful and colds away. So I did some experimenting and found that once soaked overnight they soften, making them an ideal smoothie ingredient. Add some lovely nutty, creamy almond milk, which is dairy free – and easy to get hold of I hasten to add (my local shop sells it) – and some other fresh fruit and you've got yourself a delicious, anti-ageing, cold-blasting magic potion!

Put the goji berries in a small bowl and add just enough water to cover. Cover with a lid or cling film/plastic wrap and leave to soak overnight, then drain.

Put all the ingredients in a blender and blitz for about 1 minute until completely smooth. Add a little extra almond milk if the smoothie appears too thick, which will depend on how juicy your blackberries are.

Pour into glasses, passing through a sieve/fine-mesh strainer if you prefer to leave out any seeds, and enjoy.

☀ WHY NOT TRY...

Blending goji berries to make a sauce. While I was enjoying my new-found love for soaked goji berries, I had a go at making a purée, which is pretty delicious spooned over yogurt and granola for breakfast, or even some frozen yogurt or ice cream for dessert. Here's what I do:

Soak 50g/1¾oz/½ cup goji berries overnight in just enough water to cover them, then drain. Put in a blender with a couple of handfuls of fresh or defrosted frozen berries (whatever you have in the refrigerator or freezer). Blitz well, then have a taste and add a little honey or agave syrup to sweeten if it's too tart. Strain through a sieve/fine-mesh strainer to remove any seeds, then store in the refrigerator for up to 2 days.

banana, matcha and honey smoothie

400ml/14fl oz/1²⁄₃ cups
milk (any type you like
– cows, almond, soy,
oat), chilled
2 ripe bananas (the riper
they are, the sweeter
they are), peeled
4 tsp matcha powder
½ tsp ground cinnamon
4 tsp honey
4 ice cubes

Using matcha green tea powder in a smoothie not only adds a subtle yet distinctive flavour and a fabulous colour, but also gives you a huge dose of antioxidants that will definitely jump-start your day and keep you feeling and looking healthy and happy. It's certainly not a cheap ingredient to buy, but believe me, it's a super healthy one and just a small amount has great benefits.

Put all of the ingredients in a blender and blitz for about 1 minute until completely smooth.

Pour into glasses and serve.

⁎ WHY NOT TRY...

Using matcha green tea powder to make a matcha-cino – a
brilliant short milky health boost. Heat up a small cup of
milk and mix in ½–1 teaspoon matcha powder. Give it
a good whisk (a hand-held milk frother is best for this)
until the powder has thoroughly dissolved and the milk is
frothy. Sweeten to taste with some honey. Pour into a cup
and sprinkle with a little chocolate, if you fancy a classic
cappuccino finish.

fruit and nut granola

4 tbsp melted coconut oil or rapeseed/canola oil, plus extra for greasing

2 very ripe bananas, peeled

50g/1¾oz/heaped ¼ cup pitted dates, roughly chopped

2 tsp vanilla extract

2 tsp ground cinnamon

a pinch of salt

250g/9oz/2½ cups rolled oats

115g/4oz/scant 1 cup mixed dried fruit (chopped if large), such as raisins, sultanas/ golden raisins, cranberries, cherries, apricots and figs

115g/4oz/scant 1 cup roughly chopped nut of your choice, or a mixture such as pecans, walnuts, Brazil nuts, hazelnuts, almonds and cashew nuts

75g/2½oz/⅔ cup mixed seeds, such as pumpkin, sunflower, flaxseed, chia and hemp

plain yogurt and fresh fruit, to serve

This homemade granola is all about natural, wholesome, good-for-you ingredients, and it contains no added sugar. These quantities can easily double up, which is well worth doing as once made it will store well in an airtight container. It's also a great recipe for using up open bags of dried fruit, nuts and seeds. Choose your own cocktail of flavours to add to the basic base of oats and banana, and enjoy every morning knowing there is no added sugar (did I mention that?).

Preheat the oven to 160°C/325°F/gas 2–3. Grease one or two large non-stick baking sheets with a little oil.

Put the bananas, dates, vanilla extract, cinnamon, melted coconut oil and salt in a food processor and blitz until completely smooth and creamy.

Put the oats, fruit, nuts and seeds in a large mixing bowl and stir to combine. Add the creamy banana mixture and mix well to coat everything.

Transfer the mixture to the prepared baking sheet(s) and roughly spread out with your fingers to make a single layer, keeping the lumpy texture that resembles granola.

Bake for 15 minutes, then remove the baking sheets from the oven and reduce the temperature to 110°C/225°F/gas ½. Stir the granola on the sheets and break up any large clumps. Return to the oven and cook for a further 45 minutes, turning every 15 minutes, until the granola is dry and crunchy. If you feel it is still a little soft in the middle, then cook for a further 15 minutes or so.

Remove from the oven and leave to cool completely on the baking sheets before storing in an airtight container. Serve with a dollop of plain yogurt and some fresh fruit. The granola will keep for up to 2 weeks in an airtight container, though I guarantee you will want to eat it all before then!

nuts about nuts

Up until fairly recently I pretty much took nuts for granted. Numerous partially used bags were always stacked up in my cupboard, left over from various recipes. When it came to using them again, they'd often be past their best and end up getting thrown out.

However, when I started to think about doing this book I began looking at all the basic ingredients around us that have huge health benefits. I soon realized that nuts can be utilized in so many ways and offer many health benefits, too.

nutrition

Nuts are packed full of healthy fats that are essential to our diet and heart, as well as providing protein, vitamins A, D and E, magnesium, zinc and omegas. They really are an all-round super ingredient to have and certainly shouldn't be pushed to the back of a shelf. We should try and use them to their full potential, and here are some wonderfully healthy ways of doing so…

nut milks

I'm pretty sure you'll have noticed the ever-increasing variety of dairy-free milks available in shops, with nut milks becoming very popular. Almond milk is currently the most commonly available and it's surprisingly easy to make yourself at home. And you don't have to stick to just almonds – pretty much any type of nut can be transformed into a smooth creamy milk that can be used just like dairy milk. The advantage of making your own is that it's super fresh, economical and you can be as creative as you wish with nut varieties and flavour additions. The best nuts to use are blanched (skinned) as they blend well, so almonds, cashews, macadamia, hazelnuts and peanuts are perfect. That said, nuts with skins on like walnuts, pecans, Brazil and pistachios can be made into milk but can give a slightly bitter taste so will benefit from adding a touch of sweetness, too (see below).

make your own…

So, to make your own, you need 1 cup nuts to 3 cups water. This will give you approximately 1l/35fl oz/4 cups of fresh milk.

» Soak the nuts in enough cold water to totally cover them and leave overnight or for at least 6 hours in the refrigerator.
» Drain and tip the nuts into a blender with 3 cups fresh cold water. Blitz thoroughly until it is smooth and creamy (it could be anywhere between 30 seconds and a few minutes, depending on the power of your blender).
» Pass through a sieve/strainer lined with muslin cloth/cheesecloth, sat over a large jug. Once most of the liquid has drained out, squeeze out any remaining liquid from the muslin/cheesecloth. And that is it…you have your very own nut milk. Once made, it will last for up to 1 week in the refrigerator (give it a shake before using if it separates slightly).
» You can tip the ground nuts left behind onto a baking sheet and leave to dry naturally and then use in recipes as you would ground almonds, or simply discard.

VARIATIONS TO ADD TO THE BLENDER:
» **Sweet nut milk** = add a pitted date or two, or sweeten with some maple syrup, agave syrup or honey.
» **Flavoured** = add spices such as ground cinnamon, or vanilla extract or cocoa powder.

nut cream

This is made in exactly the same way as you would make nut milk but the amount of water added to the blender is reduced, depending on the

thickness you require – so you can have smooth velvety pouring cream or thick cloud-like like whipped cream. Serve with desserts (see page 190 for Strawberries with Vanilla Cashew Cream) or use as you would a use dairy cream.

» Start off by adding 1 cup soaked blanched nuts to a blender with 1 cup cold water. Blend thoroughly until smooth and thick. Loosen with more cold water to the desired consistency.

VARIATIONS TO ADD TO THE BLENDER:
» To sweeten, add maple syrup, agave syrup or honey. Cocoa powder can also make a nice addition.
» Add flavour with extracts like vanilla, lemon, coconut or rose, or ground spices such as cinnamon, mixed spice, ginger or nutmeg.

nut butters

When growing up, a tub of peanut butter rarely lasted long in the cupboard. I loved it spread onto toast, a bagel or simply straight out of the jar (though I'd get told off if my mum saw me!). I've not lost my love for it at all — however, I am pretty conscious of how expensive it can be and that it can contain additives and preservatives, which can easily be avoided if you make your own… and to make your own it's amazingly simple. As with nut milks, any nut can be used to make butter, so you can now finish off all those opened bags of nuts and transform them into a delicious and extremely versatile spread. They can be raw or roasted (roasted gives a deeper flavour and colour) and once made will last for a couple of weeks in the refrigerator (if you can resist eating it sooner):

» Tip the nuts into a blender or food processor and blitz for about 1 minute. Scrape down the sides of the bowl and blitz again, repeating

this process for a good few minutes until you have a super-creamy, smooth paste. You can add a little olive or coconut oil to loosen the consistency if preferred, though if you persevere with the blending this shouldn't be necessary with most nuts.

VARIATIONS TO ADD TO THE BLENDER:
» Add a pinch of sea salt, or maple syrup, agave syrup or honey to taste.
» **Crunchy Nut Butter** - add an additional handful of nuts to the blended butter and blend again to reach your chosen chunkiness.
» **Cinnamon and Raisin** – add a handful of raisins and ground cinnamon to taste.
» **Choc n Nut** – add some cocoa powder and palm sugar or maple syrup.
» **Spicy Butter** – add a good pinch of dried chilli/hot pepper flakes, sea salt and a squeeze of honey.

seeds

Don't just stop at nuts – milk and butter can be made with a variety of seeds, too, including hemp, sunflower, sesame and pumpkin. You can also make your own tahini with sesame seeds. It can be costly to buy pre-made and can often taste a little bitter so why not make your own?

Put 155g/4½oz/1 cup sesame seeds, either raw or lightly toasted (for a nuttier and deeper flavour) in a food processor and blitz to a crumbly paste. Add 2 tablespoons neutral-flavoured oil such as groundnut/peanut or light olive oil and blend again to a smooth paste, adding more oil if required. Season with a pinch of salt (optional). Store in the refrigerator for a month or so.

preparation time: 15 minutes
cooking time: 5 minutes

raspberry yogurt crunch pots

40g/1½oz/scant ½ cup
   rolled oats
2 tbsp medium oatmeal
40g/1½oz/½ cup flaked/
   sliced almonds, lightly
   crushed in your hands
2 tbsp pumpkin seeds
2 tbsp sunflower seeds
1 tsp ground cinnamon
2 tbsp maple syrup
300g/10½oz/heaped
   2 cups raspberries
3 tbsp fresh orange,
   apple, cranberry or
   pomegranate juice
500g/1lb 2oz/2 cups
   low-fat Greek or plain
   yogurt, or coconut
   yogurt

The 'crunch' in these pots is a bit like a cheat's version of a granola. It won't last as long as granola – perhaps just a couple of days in an airtight container – before it loses the crunch, but it's very quick to make and really livens up a bowl of fruit and yogurt for breakfast, giving it a super-healthy boost of fibre, protein, good fats, vitamins and minerals. If you've other berries, give them a go – you certainly don't only have to stick to raspberries for this. And you also don't have to have this for breakfast – it makes a pretty good dessert, too (especially if you mix a little grated dark/bittersweet chocolate into the cooked 'crunch' before serving).

Set a frying pan over a medium heat and add the oats, oatmeal, almonds, pumpkin seeds, sunflower seeds and cinnamon. Gently toast, stirring frequently, for about 5 minutes until the oats start to turn a little golden and the pumpkin seeds start to pop. Pour in the maple syrup and toss around until the oats and seeds are coated. Remove from the heat and transfer to a shallow bowl to cool for a few minutes.

Lightly mash half of the raspberries with the fruit juice using a fork, then stir in the remaining raspberries.

Layer up the yogurt, raspberries and crunchy mixture in serving glasses, finishing with a layer of 'crunch'. Serve.

orange blossom and pistachio porridge

100g/3½oz/1 cup rolled oats

2 tbsp milled flaxseed

400ml/14fl oz/1⅔ cups almond milk, plus extra if needed

½–1 tsp orange blossom water, or to taste

1 small handful of shelled pistachio nuts, roughly chopped

agave syrup or honey, to taste

dried edible rose petals, to serve (optional)

I'm a big fan of porridge/oatmeal, especially during the colder months, and I'm always after new ways to serve it. This blew me away when I first made it. I didn't quite expect the combination of slightly nutty, creamy, almond milk, fragrant orange blossom and distinctive-flavoured pistachio nuts to work so well in a porridge/oatmeal. If it hadn't been so filling, I'd have gone in for a second serving. The rose petals are optional, but not only do they look pretty, they also add a mildly floral flavour to this divine dish.

Put the oats, flaxseed and almond milk in a non-stick saucepan and gently bring to a simmer over a medium heat. Cook, stirring occasionally, for 4–5 minutes until the oats are tender and creamy. If the porridge/oatmeal is too thick, add a little more milk, as needed. Stir in the orange blossom water. Different brands vary in strength, so add a little at a time — you are after a subtle flavour, not anything too overpowering.

Spoon equally into bowls, scatter over the pistachios and add agave syrup or honey to taste. Serve with a sprinkling of rose petals, if you like.

* **PS...** If you don't have any orange blossom water, a little orange zest can be used instead. You will get a very different flavour – but it's still very tasty. Or sticking to a floral theme, a little rosewater can be added, if you happen to have any.

2 small or 1 large ripe
   pear
75g/2½oz/¾ cup rolled
   oats
4 tbsp quinoa flakes
2 tbsp milled flaxseed
1 tsp ground cinnamon,
   plus extra, for dusting
400ml/14fl oz/1⅔ cups
   milk, plus extra if
   needed
agave syrup or honey,
   to taste

pear and cinnamon porridge

Adding fresh pear to this porridge/oatmeal gives a light refreshing flavour and a natural sweetness – and is a good way to use up any pears you have that are past their best. There's also the added benefit of quinoa flakes in with the oats. They add a subtle nuttiness and, of course, all the goodness that quinoa is known for – like amino acids and protein and vitamins and iron and … the list is endless – it's not known as a superfood for no good reason. It's not essential to use quinoa in the recipe, however. If you don't have any, just increase the oats by 25g/1oz/¼ cup.

Coarsely grate the pears, leaving just the cores behind, and put into a non-stick saucepan. You can peel the pears first if you like, but they retain more goodness if left unpeeled.

Add the oats, quinoa flakes, flaxseed, cinnamon and about three-quarters of the milk and gently bring to a simmer over a medium heat. Cook, stirring occasionally, for about 5 minutes until the oats are tender and creamy. If the porridge/oatmeal is too thick, add a little more milk as needed.

Spoon equally into bowls and drizzle with agave syrup or honey to taste. Serve with a dusting of cinnamon.

ginger berry muffins

MAKES 10
preparation time: 10 minutes, plus making the apple purée (optional)
cooking time: 30 minutes

225g/8oz/1¾ cups wholemeal/whole-wheat flour

2 tsp baking powder

½ tsp bicarbonate of soda/baking soda

150ml/5fl oz/scant ⅔ cup plain yogurt

3 tbsp melted coconut oil or rapeseed/canola oil

125ml/4fl oz/½ cup unsweetened apple sauce or apple purée (see below)

6 tbsp agave syrup or honey

2 tsp finely grated root ginger

finely grated zest of ½ orange

200g/7oz/1⅓–1½ cups fresh berries, such as blueberries, small raspberries or small blackberries

Sugar-free muffins? 'What's the point?', I hear you shout. Well, these fruity little things are still, in my book, a treat. All the fruit ingredients make them sweet enough and the fresh ginger gives your taste buds a nice little kick. So, there's nothing to miss — get your aprons on people and start baking.

Preheat the oven to 180°C/350°F/gas 4. Line a muffin pan with 10 paper or silicone muffin cases.

Combine the flour, baking powder and bicarbonate of soda/baking soda in a large mixing bowl.

In a separate bowl or jug, mix together all the remaining ingredients, except the berries.

Add the wet ingredients to the dry and briefly mix, still leaving plenty of lumps in the batter as this will result in lighter muffins. Gently fold in the berries. Spoon the batter equally into the muffin cases and lightly smooth over the surfaces with the back of the spoon.

Bake for 25–30 minutes, or until golden and just firm to touch. Leave to cool in the pan for a few minutes before serving warm or transferring to a wire/cooling rack to cool completely.

*HOW TO MAKE: APPLE PURÉE

Ready-made unsweetened fruit purées are becoming more widely available as they are a great way of adding a natural sweetness to baking. However, it is really easy to make your own apple purée for this recipe, and any left over will keep in the refrigerator for a few days or can be frozen.

Put 450g/1lb peeled, cored and chopped eating apples in a saucepan along with 125ml/4fl oz/½ cup water. Bring to a simmer over a medium heat, then reduce the heat to medium-low, cover with a lid and cook for about 15 minutes until the apple has completely broken down, stirring occasionally. When the apple is soft, beat until smooth or blitz with a hand-held/immersion blender.

banana and date muffins

MAKES 8-10

preparation time: 20 minutes
cooking time: 20 minutes

75g/2½oz/heaped ⅓ cup pitted dates, roughly chopped

125ml/4fl oz/½ cup black Earl Grey tea

½ tsp bicarbonate of soda/baking soda

2 very ripe bananas, peeled

I egg

125ml/4fl oz/½ cup buttermilk

I tsp vanilla extract

125g/4½oz/¾ cup plus I tbsp wholemeal/ whole-wheat flour

50g/1¾oz/½ cup ground almonds

1½ tsp baking powder

I tsp ground cinnamon

The riper the bananas the sweeter the taste, so don't go throwing out bananas that don't look their best – they're perfect for this recipe. Once made, you should eat the muffins within a day or two as they can go a little dry because there is no added sugar and very little fat in the recipe. You can get an extra day out of them by warming them through in the oven or microwave or serving them with a drizzle of honey, agave or maple syrup. I've kept these ones plain, but it is quite nice to add some chopped walnuts or pecans to the batter, or even some additional diced banana, which sweetens them up even more.

Put the dates and tea in a small saucepan and bring to the boil. Remove from the heat and stir in the bicarbonate of soda/baking soda. Leave to cool for about 10 minutes until it is lukewarm.

Meanwhile, preheat the oven to 200°C/400°F/gas 6. Line a muffin pan with paper or silicone muffin cases. (I like to make 8 slightly larger muffins but you can make 10 medium-size ones if you prefer.)

Put the bananas in a food processor and whizz until puréed. Add the egg, buttermilk and vanilla extract and whizz together until it forms a creamy batter.

Mix in the date and tea mixture and all of the remaining ingredients and blend until only just combined. Try not to overmix the muffin batter as they will be lighter in texture when only just mixed.

Spoon the batter equally into the prepared muffin cases. Bake for 18–20 minutes, or until golden and just firm to touch. Leave to cool in the pan for a few minutes before serving warm or transferring to a wire/cooling rack to cool completely.

PS... While they are still nice and fresh, I quite like to serve these as a dessert with some sliced fresh pineapple, a drizzle of maple syrup and a dollop of Greek yogurt. A simple, tasty and healthy end to any meal.

apple, cranberry and walnut gluten-free loaf

oil, for greasing

350g/12oz/2⅔ cups buckwheat flour

1 tsp bicarbonate of soda/ baking soda

1 tsp ground cinnamon

½ tsp salt

2 apples, peeled, cored and coarsely grated

75g/2½oz/⅔ cup dried cranberries, roughly chopped

75g/2½oz/¾ cup walnuts, roughly chopped

250ml/9fl oz/1 cup fresh apple juice

1 egg, lightly beaten

50g/1¾oz/3½ tbsp butter, melted

2 tbsp honey

1 tbsp gluten-free rolled oats

This is something for breakfast that will keep you full until lunch, or a little treat to have as an energy boost in the middle of the afternoon. I love it straight from the oven with a little butter or jam, or toasted with a dollop of ricotta cheese and honey. Once it's made, it will last a good few days if wrapped in paper or foil – mind you, it won't be around long.

Preheat the oven to 180°C/350°F/gas 4 and lightly oil a 1kg/2lb 4oz loaf pan.

Combine the flour, bicarbonate of soda/baking soda, cinnamon and salt in a large mixing bowl. Stir in the grated apples and chopped cranberries and walnuts, reserving a small amount of the walnuts to scatter over the top of the loaf.

In a separate bowl or jug, mix together the apple juice, egg, melted butter and honey, then pour into the bowl with the flour. Gently mix together, making sure you don't overmix so that you have a lighter loaf when cooked.

Spoon the mixture into the prepared loaf pan. Scatter the reserved walnuts and the oats over the top. Bake for 40–45 minutes, or until the top is lightly golden and a skewer inserted into the middle of the loaf comes out clean. Leave to cool in the pan for 10 minutes before serving warm or turning out onto a wire/cooling rack to cool completely.

PS... Feel free to ring the changes with this loaf to suit your preferences. Grated pears can be used instead of the apples, and equal weights of pretty much any dried fruit and nuts can be swapped for the cranberries and walnuts. One of my other favourite combinations is pear, cherry and pecan.

buckwheat and coconut crêpes with baked figs

200g/7oz/1½ cups
   buckwheat flour
450ml/16fl oz/2 cups
   milk, plus extra if
   needed
2 eggs
a pinch of salt
finely grated zest of
   1 orange
2 tbsp melted coconut
   oil, plus extra for frying
50g/1¾oz/½ cup
   unsweetened desiccated/
   dried shredded coconut
Greek yogurt, to serve
   (optional)

For the figs:
8–10 figs, depending on
   their size
4 tbsp honey
125ml/4fl oz/½ cup
   freshly squeezed orange
   juice

In addition to the delicious nutty flavour that buckwheat flour gives these crêpes, it also makes them high in fibre and gluten free, not to mention rich in nutrients, including calcium, protein, iron and B vitamins. So all in all, it's pretty good for you and makes pretty tasty crêpes, especially when mixed with some dried coconut. They can be served as simply as you like – adding just a squeeze of lemon and a drizzle of honey (my daughter Rosa's favourite), dripping with maple syrup (my son Olly's favourite) or you can posh them up a bit and serve with Greek yogurt and sticky figs baked with orange juice (my favourite). Enjoy.

Preheat the oven to 200°C/400°F/gas 6.

Trim the stalks off the figs and cut each one in half. Put in a small roasting pan and drizzle the honey over the top. Pour over the orange juice and bake for 20 minutes, basting with the orange juice a couple of times during cooking. When cooked, serve hot, warm or cooled. Keep the figs warm while you make the crêpes, or leave them to cool, if you like.

To make the crêpes, put all of the ingredients except the coconut and yogurt in a food processor and blitz until smooth. The consistency should be similar to thick pouring cream. Stir in the coconut and add a little extra milk if needed to return the batter to the correct consistency.

Preheat the oven to its lowest setting. Heat a non-stick frying pan over a medium-high heat. When hot, add a trickle of oil and use a brush to evenly coat the pan. Pour in just enough of the batter to cover the surface, swirling the pan to get an even coating. Cook for about 1–2 minutes until lightly golden. Flip over using a spatula and cook for about 1 minute, or until golden, on the other side. Keep warm in the oven while cooking the rest. You should make about 8 crêpes.

Serve the crêpes with the figs, spooning over any sticky orange juices. Serve with Greek yogurt, if you like.

SERVES 4

preparation time: 10 minutes
cooking time: 20 minutes

banana and spelt pancakes with blueberry compôte

200g/7oz/1½ cups
 wholegrain spelt flour
2 tbsp flaxseed
2 tsp baking powder
1 tsp ground cinnamon
a pinch of salt
2 eggs
2 very ripe bananas,
 peeled and roughly
 chopped
250ml/9fl oz/1 cup milk
2 tbsp melted coconut
 oil, plus extra for frying

For the blueberry compôte:
200g/7oz/1½ cups
 blueberries
1 peeled strip of lemon
 zest
1 tbsp agave syrup or
 maple syrup

To serve:
honey, maple syrup or
 agave syrup
Greek yogurt or coconut
 yogurt (optional)

Spelt is a fantastic flour to use as an alternative to wheat flour, and can be especially helpful for those who have a mild wheat intolerance. This is due to the fact that the gluten in spelt flour is water soluble, making it far more digestible. I quite like to use wholegrain spelt flour for these delicious pancakes, for added fibre and goodness, but white spelt or in fact standard wheat flour, white or wholemeal/whole-wheat, can of course be used instead.

Start by making the blueberry compôte. Put the blueberries in a small saucepan with 1 tablespoon water, the lemon zest and syrup. Cook over a medium heat for 2–3 minutes until the berries burst and release their juices. Remove from the heat and leave to cool.

To make the pancakes, put the flour, flaxseed, baking powder, cinnamon and salt in a food processor and whizz briefly to mix and get some air into the dry ingredients.

Add the eggs, bananas, milk and melted coconut oil. Whizz until it forms a smooth pancake batter.

Preheat the oven to its lowest setting. Heat a non-stick frying pan (or two) over a medium-low heat, add a little coconut oil and swirl around to coat the base and sides of the pan. Spoon 3–4 spoonfuls of the pancake batter into the pan, spacing them well apart, and cook for 2–3 minutes until they are starting to dry out around the edges and a few small bubbles appear on the surface. Carefully turn them over with a spatula and continue to cook for about 1 minute on the other side until golden. Keep warm in the oven while cooking the rest. You should make about 12 pancakes.

Serve the pancakes piled up with the blueberry compôte spooned over. Add a drizzle of honey and a spoonful of yogurt, if you like.

roast mushrooms and avocado on rye

SERVES 4

preparation time: 15 minutes
cooking time: 40 minutes

4 large portobello
  mushrooms
olive or rapeseed/canola
  oil, for rubbing
2 ripe avocados, peeled
  and pitted
juice and zest of
  ½ lemon
1 tbsp chopped flat leaf
  parsley leaves
1 tbsp extra virgin olive
  oil
4 thick slices of rye bread
sea salt and freshly
  ground black pepper

For the toasted seeds:
125g/4½oz/1 cup mixed
  seeds, such as pumpkin,
  sunflower, chia, sesame,
  flaxseed and hemp
1 tsp rapeseed/canola oil
1 tsp soy sauce
1 tsp agave syrup
a pinch of cayenne
  pepper

Rye bread has less wheat than many other breads, which is a benefit to many, but I've suggested it here as it has a delicious flavour that works brilliantly with the toasted seeds. That said, don't feel you have to stick to using it. Any bread can be used, including soda bread and (my favourite) walnut bread. This makes more than enough toasted seeds for the breakfast recipe, but it is well worth making this amount as you can use them to sprinkle on salads, soups or just to nibble on throughout the day. Once made, the seed mix will last for up to three weeks in an airtight container.

Preheat the oven to 190°C/375°F/gas 5 and line a baking sheet with baking parchment. Mix together all of the toasted seed ingredients, then spread the mixture flat on the prepared baking sheet. Bake for 15–20 minutes until dry and golden, stirring halfway through. Remove from the oven and leave to cool. Turn the oven up to 200°C/400°F/gas 6.

Put the mushrooms on a baking sheet and rub a little olive oil into each one. Season with salt and pepper and roast for 20 minutes, or until they are tender and are just starting to release their juices.

Meanwhile, mash the avocados with a fork until fairly smooth. Stir in the lemon zest and juice, parsley and extra virgin olive oil, and season with salt and pepper.

Lightly toast the bread. Divide the avocado mixture onto the slices, then top with the roasted mushrooms, either leaving whole or slicing first. Scatter with toasted seeds and serve.

poached eggs, tahini and pan-fried avocado

SERVES 4 (or 2 very hungry people)
preparation time: 10 minutes
cooking time: 5 minutes

2 tbsp white wine vinegar

4 eggs

2 tbsp olive or coconut oil

2 ripe avocados, peeled, pitted and cut into 1cm/½in thick slices

4 thick slices of fresh bread (such as sourdough or rye bread)

3 tbsp tahini, plus extra to serve

1 tsp sumac

1 tsp toasted sesame seeds

sea salt and freshly ground black pepper

extra virgin olive oil, for drizzling

I love this recipe – it's simple to prepare, completely satisfying (especially if you've slightly overdone it the night before) and looks pretty impressive, too. Rather than using bought, processed sliced bread, I recommend a crustier loaf such as farmhouse, sourdough or rye. Once toasted, the crunch you get from them works really well with the soft egg and avocado. As for the tahini – it really tops off the dish. This protein-rich paste made from ground sesame seeds gives some real oomph. If you've not already tried pan-frying avocado, then you must give this recipe a go. It has a smoky taste, similar to that of mild smoked bacon, so it's perfect with eggs for a late breakfast or brunch.

Bring a medium to large pan of water to the boil over a medium-high heat and add the white wine vinegar. Break in the eggs one at a time and reduce the heat to a gentle simmer. Cook for 2–3 minutes until the whites are set.

Meanwhile, heat the olive oil in a large frying pan. Add the avocado slices and fry for about 1–2 minutes on each side until slightly golden. Remove from the heat and season with salt and pepper.

Toast the bread until golden. Spread each slice with tahini, then top with the avocado slices. Remove the poached eggs from the pan with a slotted spoon. Dry any excess water with paper towels and then put the eggs on top of the toasts. Season with salt and pepper. Scatter with the sumac and sesame seeds, then serve with a drizzle of extra virgin olive oil and a little more tahini.

turmeric and coriander omelettes with chilli tomatoes

6 eggs

1 tsp ground turmeric

2 tbsp chopped
coriander/cilantro
leaves

4 tsp olive oil

For the chilli tomatoes:

4 tsp olive oil

200g/7oz/1½ cups cherry
tomatoes, halved

2 garlic cloves, crushed

a pinch of dried chilli/
hot pepper flakes

1 tsp nigella seeds

2 large handfuls of
spinach leaves, roughly
chopped

sea salt and freshly
ground black pepper

This is certainly a breakfast or brunch dish that's not lacking in flavour or colour, and is guaranteed to impress whoever you make it for. Turmeric gives the omelette a vibrant yellow colour and a mellow spiced flavour, and is said to have powerful anti-inflammatory and antioxidant properties that could potentially ward off some pretty horrible things. When it comes to making omelettes, I would always suggest you make one for each person, rather then a large omelette to share. It makes a lighter omelette and it's easier to turn out of the pan.

To make the chilli tomatoes, heat a frying pan over a medium heat and add the oil. When hot, add the tomatoes and garlic. Fry for a couple of minutes until the tomatoes start to soften, then stir in the dried chilli/hot pepper flakes and nigella seeds and season with salt and pepper. Continue to cook for 2–3 minutes until the tomatoes are squishy. Finally, stir in the spinach until it's wilted, then keep warm while you make the omelettes.

Beat the eggs in a bowl, add the turmeric and coriander/cilantro, and season with salt and pepper.

Heat a small non-stick frying pan over a medium-high heat. Add half the oil and swirl around to coat the base and sides of the pan. Pour half of the egg mixture into the pan. Move around in the pan with the base of a fork (taking care not to scratch your pan) until you have a soft scrambled consistency. Now leave the omelette to finish cooking so the egg is just set – this should only take a minute or so. Keep warm while you make the second omelette with the remaining egg mixture.

Transfer the omelettes to plates. Spoon half of the chilli tomatoes and spinach onto one side of each omelette, then fold the other half of the omelette over the top. Serve hot.

korean courgette pancakes with smoked salmon

SERVES 4

preparation time: 20 minutes

cooking time: 20–40 minutes

1 egg

200g/7oz/1½ cups wholemeal/whole-wheat flour

2 tbsp toasted sesame seeds, plus extra to serve

1 tsp salt

450g/1lb courgettes/ zucchini, coarsely grated

olive or rapeseed/canola oil, for frying

toasted sesame oil, for drizzling

8–12 slices of smoked salmon, depending on their size

For the dipping sauce:

2 tbsp soy sauce

2 tbsp rice vinegar

2 tsp toasted sesame oil

a pinch of dried chilli/ hot pepper flakes

This is my take on a popular Korean dish. It's a crispy savoury pancake packed with courgettes/zucchini. I use wholemeal/whole-wheat flour rather than plain/all-purpose flour and add sesame seeds to an egg-and-water mix for a healthier touch. I serve the pancakes with some brain-boosting smoked salmon (not traditional) to turn this into a very tasty brunch dish. That said, it works well served any time of the day.

Lightly beat the egg in a large mixing bowl. Add the flour, sesame seeds, salt and 250ml/9fl oz/1 cup water. Mix to form a thick batter and leave to rest for 5 minutes.

Mix together all the ingredients for the dipping sauce and pour into small dishes.

Preheat the oven to its lowest setting. Add the grated courgette/zucchini to the pancake batter and mix well.

Heat a large frying pan over a medium-high heat and add enough oil to coat the surface. (If you've two pans, I'd recommend getting two pancakes cooking at a time to speed things up.) Spoon a quarter of the batter into the pan and spread out with the back of a spoon to make a large pancake. Cook for 4–5 minutes until golden and crispy. The top should now be dried out so, if you can, flip the pancake over by tossing the pan (taking care no oil splashes you), or carefully turn using a spatula. Alternatively, you can slide the pancake onto a plate and invert it back into the pan to cook the other side.

Cook for a further 3–4 minutes, then trickle some sesame oil around the edge of the pancake, to give it an authentic sesame flavour, and cook for a final 30 seconds or so. If you feel the pancake is a little doughy in the middle, continue cooking, pressing down with a spatula, until set and dry to the touch. Keep warm in the oven while cooking the rest.

Serve the pancakes whole or cut into wedges with slices of smoked salmon, the dipping sauce and a sprinkling of toasted sesame seeds.

light meals

SERVES 4

preparation time: 30 minutes,
plus 1 hour macerating
cooking time: 10 minutes

warm duck and cherry salad

300g/10½oz/1½ cups
   juicy ripe cherries
3 tbsp extra virgin olive
   oil
2 tsp red wine vinegar
2 tbsp kirsch (cherry
   liqueur)
8 juniper berries, lightly
   crushed
50g/1¾oz/heaped ½ cup
   flaked/sliced almonds
2 large duck breasts, skin
   and fat removed
olive oil, for frying
50g/1¾oz/1⅔ cups baby
   watercress leaves
1 large handful of mint
   leaves, roughly chopped
zest of 1 lemon
sea salt and freshly
   ground black pepper

Cherries are naturally lower in sugars than many fruits and have wonderful anti-inflammatory and antioxidant properties, so it's well worth making the most of them during the summer months when they're at their best, and their cheapest. This salad is a great sharing first course for a relaxed summery lunch or dinner party and you can prepare most of the recipe in advance – it's simply the duck that needs cooking just before you serve. However, that said, you can serve it cold if you wish, cutting down on any last minute cooking.

To prepare the cherries, break each cherry apart with your fingers and remove the pits. Put in bowl along with the extra virgin olive oil, vinegar, kirsch and juniper berries. Gently mix together and leave at room temperature for about 1 hour to macerate, stirring occasionally, then remove the juniper berries.

Heat a frying pan over a medium heat and toast the almonds for a few minutes, stirring occasionally, until they are light golden. Remove from the pan and leave to cool.

Preheat the oven to 220°C/425°F/gas 7. Season the duck breasts with salt and pepper. Heat a frying pan over a high heat. Add a trickle of olive oil and when hot, quickly brown the duck for about 1 minute on each side until deep golden. Remove from the pan and transfer to a small roasting pan. Transfer to the oven to finish cooking for 5 minutes. (After this time, the duck should be cooked medium-rare. If you prefer a more well-done piece of meat, leave to cook for a minute or two longer.) Remove from the oven, cover the pan with foil and leave to rest.

Toss the watercress and mint into the cherries and put on a serving plate. Thinly slice the duck and put on top. Spoon over any resting juices from the roasting pan, plus any dressing left in the bottom of the cherry bowl. Serve scattered with the toasted almonds and lemon zest.

poached chicken and spring green broth

1–1.2kg/2lb 4oz–2lb 12oz
   whole chicken
2 leeks, roughly chopped
2 carrots, roughly
   chopped
2 celery stalks, roughly
   chopped
4 garlic cloves
2 bay leaves
2 tsp salt

For the broth:
150g/5½oz spring/
   collard greens, finely
   sliced
125g/4½oz/heaped
   ¾ cup frozen peas,
   defrosted
8 spring onions/
   scallions, chopped
4 tbsp low-fat crème
   fraîche or sour cream
finely grated zest of
   ½ lemon
1 large handful of fresh
   chervil, basil, mint or
   chives, roughly chopped
sea salt and freshly
   ground black pepper

Spring/collard greens are bundles of green goodness that are the ideal antidote to overindulging during the winter months. As soon as spring has sprung, so do the greens. They're part of the Brassica family (which includes cabbage, cauliflower, kale, broccoli and Brussels sprouts) and have a silky soft texture and sweet flavour that lends itself perfectly to a light and flavoursome poached chicken broth. As for their health benefits, well, you really can't eat enough of them. They provide you with a seriously useful amount of vitamin C, to support your immune system, and vitamin K to build bone strength, not to mention natural compounds with anti-inflammatory and anti-cancer properties.

Put the chicken into a large saucepan with the leeks, carrots, celery, garlic, bay leaves and salt. Cover completely with about 2.5l/84fl oz/10½ cups cold water and bring to the boil over a high heat. As soon as it boils, reduce the heat to medium-low and skim away any scum on the surface with a metal spoon. Loosely cover with a lid and leave to gently simmer for 2 hours until tender. Carefully lift the chicken from the pan onto a plate. Cover with foil and keep hot.

Strain the stock left in the pan through a sieve/strainer into a couple of large jugs. Skim away any fat that rises to the surface. Pour about 1.5l/52fl oz/6¼ cups of the stock into a wide-based saucepan and bring to the boil over a high heat. Leave the liquid to reduce to about 750ml/26fl oz/3 cups. (Any remaining stock from poaching the chicken can be left to cool, then refrigerated or frozen, and you'll have a delicious homemade stock to use in other recipes.)

Meanwhile, take the meat off the chicken and break into fairly chunky pieces. It will literally fall off the bone as it will be so tender.

When the stock has reduced, add the spring/collard greens to the pan and leave to cook for 3 minutes until just tender. Add the peas, spring onions/scallions and chicken. Return to a simmer and cook for about 2 minutes, then stir in the crème fraîche, lemon zest and herbs. Season with salt and pepper, ladle into bowls and serve.

asian chicken, noodle and mango salad

SERVES 4

preparation time: 25 minutes, plus 30 minutes standing (optional)

cooking time: 15 minutes

2 skinless, boneless chicken breast fillets

100g/3½oz dried glass or vermicelli noodles

2 green-skinned (under-ripe) mangoes, peeled

1 large carrot, peeled

½ cucumber, halved and deseeded

1 small red pepper, deseeded and very thinly sliced

1 small red onion, finely sliced

1 handful of coriander/cilantro leaves, roughly chopped

1 handful of mint leaves, roughly chopped

1 handful of Thai basil leaves (or standard sweet basil), roughly chopped

50g/1¾oz/heaped ⅓ cup roasted unsalted peanuts, chopped

sea salt

For the chilli lime dressing:

4 tbsp lime juice

2 tbsp fish sauce

2 tbsp palm sugar or soft brown sugar

1 red bird's eye chilli, finely sliced

2 garlic cloves, crushed

This is such a great salad for when you're in the mood for something totally light and refreshing with a spicy kick to it. You can use leftover roast chicken for the salad but I prefer to poach the chicken as and when I need it. It's a great low-fat method of cooking that ensures the meat will stay nice and juicy. For a touch of sweetness, I've added fresh mango in the salad, but try and buy green-skinned, firm mangoes for this – the type you'd often buy and wait to ripen up at home. If they are too ripe and juicy, they won't cut into strips and will become mushy. It's best not to put them in at all if they are too ripe.

Put the chicken in a saucepan in a single layer and pour over water to come about 2.5cm/1in above the chicken. Add a pinch of salt, set the pan over a medium-high heat and bring to the boil. Cover with a lid, reduce the heat to low and simmer for 5 minutes. Take the pan off the heat and leave the chicken in the pan for 10 minutes until cooked through. Scoop the chicken out with a slotted spoon and transfer to a board to cool.

Return the poaching liquid to the boil, add the noodles and remove from the heat. Leave to soak for about 4 minutes, or until tender, and then drain. Cool under cold running water, drain well and put in a large mixing bowl.

Ideally using a julienne peeler, slice the mango, carrot and cucumber into thin matchsticks. Add to the noodles with the red pepper, red onion and herbs. Shred the cooled chicken and add to the salad.

Mix together all the dressing ingredients until the sugar has dissolved, then pour over the salad. Toss the salad well and leave to stand for about 30 minutes or more, if you have the time, to allow the dressing to really flavour the salad. Just before serving, scatter over the peanuts.

※ PS... A good tip for getting thin, even julienned carrots, cucumber and mango is to use a serrated vegetable peeler, julienne peeler or a mandoline. If you don't have one, it will just be a little more time-consuming in the preparation, but believe me the end result is well worth it.

SERVES 4
preparation time: 25 minutes,
plus at least 30 minutes
marinating
cooking time: 40 minutes

ginger chicken with cucumber and celery slaw

8 large skinless chicken
   thighs, bone in
70g/2½oz root ginger,
   peeled and grated
2 garlic cloves, crushed
finely grated zest of
   ½ orange
1 tbsp harissa paste
½ tsp ground cinnamon
3 tbsp honey
1 tbsp orange blossom
   water

*For the cucumber and celery
   slaw:*
½ cucumber, sliced
   lengthways, deseeded
   and thinly sliced
4 celery stalks, very thinly
   sliced
¼ white cabbage, thinly
   shredded
4 spring onions/
   scallions, finely sliced
3 tbsp tahini
3 tbsp lemon juice
1 tbsp extra virgin olive
   oil
2 tsp sumac
sea salt and freshly
   ground black pepper

These chicken thighs are marinated in a pretty powerful combination of ingredients. There's a fantastic firey kick from the spicy harissa paste and the large amount of super-healthy ginger. Yet it's not overpowering as it's nicely balanced out with the sweet honey, fragrant orange and aromatic cinnamon. When I first made this dish, I served it hot from the oven, with cooling crunchy coleslaw, but it is just as delicious served cold the next day as the flavours seem to get better and better.

To prepare the chicken, slash each thigh 2–3 times with a sharp knife and put in a non-reactive bowl. Mix together the remaining chicken ingredients and pour over the thighs. Make sure the chicken is evenly coated, cover and leave to marinate in the refrigerator for 30–60 minutes.

Meanwhile, you can make the slaw. Put all of the vegetables into a large bowl and toss together. In a separate bowl, mix together the tahini, lemon juice, olive oil, sumac, salt, pepper and 1 tablespoon water. Pour over the vegetables and toss everything together to thoroughly combine. Leave to stand for about 30 minutes, or longer, for the dressing to soak into the vegetables.

When you are ready to cook, preheat the oven to 180°C/350°F/gas 4. Remove the chicken from the marinade and put in an ovenproof dish or baking pan just big enough so that the chicken pieces are quite close together. Pour over half of the marinade and roast for 20 minutes. Baste with the juices in the dish and spoon over some more of the raw marinade. Return to the oven for a further 20 minutes, until golden and cooked through, basting a couple more times with the juices in the pan, not the raw marinade – this can now be discarded.

Serve the chicken hot or cold with the cucumber and celery slaw.

SERVES 4

preparation time: 10 minutes

melon and parma ham salad with ginger dressing

500g/1lb 2oz juicy, ripe
  melon flesh, at room
  temperature
12 slices of Parma ham/
  prosciutto

For the ginger dressing:
2cm/¾in piece of root
  ginger, peeled and
  roughly chopped
finely grated zest of
  ½ lemon
a pinch of salt
1 tbsp lemon juice
2 tbsp extra virgin olive
  oil
2 tsp honey
½ tsp freshly ground
  black pepper

My mum would make made this salad a lot when I was growing up, and it was always a winner. For the dressing she used stem ginger in syrup, but it is very sweet, especially for a healthy cookbook, so I played around using fresh root ginger. Ginger is known for its anti-inflammatory and anti-nausea properties. The fresh ginger dressing hits the right spot – it's a little firey, a touch sweet, tangy and perfectly peppery. Just the right match for the sweet juicy melon and salty Parma ham/prosciutto. I like to use a selection of melon varieties such as Galia, Charentais, Cantaloupe or Honeydew, which gives a nice bit of colour to the plate as well as flavour, but you can stick to just one – just make sure that whatever you use, it is juicy, ripe and served at room temperature.

To make the dressing, put the ginger, lemon zest and salt in a pestle and mortar and pound to make a paste. Add the lemon juice, olive oil, honey and pepper and mix well.

Chop the melon into slices or chunks, then transfer to plates and divide the slices of Parma ham/prosciutto evenly among them. Spoon over the dressing and serve.

＊WHY NOT TRY...

Using fresh ginger to make tea. It is such a healthy ingredient, being good not only for your digestion but also for your circulation and it is also said to be a great antioxidant. On days when I am working from home, I'll often make a big pot of ginger tea to sip on, and what I don't drink hot, I'll chill in the refrigerator and serve as an iced tea the following day.

Put 2 tablespoons peeled and freshly grated root ginger in a clean teapot or large jug. Pour over 1l/35fl oz/4 cups boiling water and leave to infuse for 10 minutes. You can add a stick of cinnamon or a few fresh mint leaves, too, if you fancy. Strain through a sieve/fine-mesh strainer into another jug and stir in the juice of 1 lemon. Add honey or agave syrup to taste, if you like it a bit sweeter, and enjoy hot, or chilled over the next couple of days.

SERVES 4

preparation time: 25 minutes,
plus 45 minutes soaking
cooking time: 30 minutes

swedish pork meatballs with goji berry sauce

50g/1¾oz/⅓ cup
   medium oatmeal
60ml/2fl oz/¼ cup milk
300g/10½oz lean
   minced/ground pork
1 tbsp chopped dill
   fronds
1 tbsp chopped parsley
   leaves
½ tsp ground allspice
1 tsp salt
finely grated zest of
   ½ lemon
2 tbsp olive oil
sea salt and freshly
   ground black pepper

For the goji berry sauce:
100g/3½oz/scant 1 cup
   dried goji berries
75g/2½oz/¾ cup dried
   cranberries
2 tbsp maple syrup
2.5cm/1in piece of root
   ginger, peeled and
   grated
zest of ½ lemon

For the cucumber-dill salad:
½ cucumber, cut into
   1cm/½in dice
1 large handful of dill,
   roughly chopped
2 tbsp low-fat crème
   fraîche
a squeeze of lemon juice

First of all — get the furniture outlet out of your mind. Thank you! Now, onto the recipe itself; every element (meatballs, sauce and salad) is full of flavour and goodness in its own right and when served together you are in for a real treat. If you happen to have any of the anti-ageing, immune-boosting sauce left over, it can be kept in the refrigerator for a good couple of weeks. It's pretty tasty in a sandwich with sliced chicken or turkey, mayo and lettuce. It will also go down very well as an alternative cranberry sauce to serve with your festive roast turkey.

First, make the sauce. Put the goji berries and cranberries in a saucepan and cover with 250ml/9fl oz/1 cup warm water. Leave to soak for about 45 minutes.

Meanwhile, put the oatmeal in a mixing bowl and stir in the milk. Leave for about 15 minutes for the milk to soak into the oatmeal, softening it.

When the oatmeal has absorbed the milk, add all the remaining meatball ingredients except the oil and season with salt and pepper. Roll into about 24 walnut-size balls. Put on a plate, cover with cling film/plastic wrap and chill for about 30 minutes.

Add the maple syrup, ginger and lemon zest to the berries and set over a medium heat. Bring to a simmer and cook for 15 minutes until the berries are plumped up and there is very little liquid in the pan. Using a hand-held/immersion blender, blitz until you have a smooth, jammy consistency. Transfer to a bowl to cool.

To make the salad, simply mix everything together in a large bowl and season with a pinch of salt. Leave to one side.

To cook the meatballs, heat a large frying pan over a medium-low heat and add the olive oil. When hot, gently fry the meatballs for 10 minutes, turning frequently, until they are golden and cooked through. Serve with a spoonful of sauce and the salad.

beef carpaccio with rocket and alfalfa salad

SERVES 4

preparation time: 10 minutes, plus at least 30 minutes chilling

cooking time: 2 minutes

olive oil, for rubbing
350g/12oz beef fillet
75g/2½oz/2 cups rocket/ arugula leaves
30g/1oz/½ cup alfalfa sprouts
Parmesan cheese shavings
sea salt and freshly ground black pepper

For the truffle dressing:
2½ tbsp truffle-infused oil or extra virgin olive oil
2 tsp red wine vinegar
½ tsp wholegrain mustard
a pinch of sugar

This is a fantastic dinner party first course as you can pretty much prepare everything in advance. It looks really impressive and the flavours are amazing. The truffle oil in the dressing adds an earthy and 'expensive' flavour to the salad. It's fairly easy to get hold of nowadays and I really do recommend using it. However, if you want an alternative, a good extra virgin olive oil or even some avocado oil will be delicious. As for the beef, I prefer to sear it first rather than serving completely raw, as you'll see many other carpaccio recipes do. This adds a nice texture and additional flavour to the dish, but you can of course keep the beef raw if you wish. My additional healthy element to this low-fat, high-protein, iron-rich dish is alfalfa sprouts. They contain a concentrated amount of various vitamins and minerals, such as calcium, vitamin K and vitamin C, and really add a fabulous flavour to this impressive dish.

Rub a little olive oil into the beef fillet and season well with salt and pepper.

Heat a frying pan over a high heat and, when smoking hot, add the beef. Sear for 1½–2 minutes maximum, turning frequently to ensure even browning. Remove from the pan to a plate and leave to rest for 1 minute. Wrap the beef tightly in a piece of cling film/plastic wrap, keeping a nice round shape, and chill for 30–60 minutes.

To make the dressing, mix together all of the ingredients in a small bowl and season with salt and pepper.

When you are ready to serve, remove the beef from the refrigerator and slice as thinly as you can using a sharp knife. Arrange on plates.

Put the rocket/arugula and alfalfa sprouts in a large bowl and toss well with the dressing. Divide evenly onto the plates and top with a few shavings of Parmesan cheese.

super sprouts

If you are not familiar with sprouts (and I don't mean Brussels sprouts - they are a different thing all together!) then do read on. I must admit I didn't used to take that much notice of the tubs of loose tangles of pale threads with tiny unopened peas/buds at the top until I realized just how amazingly good for you they are.

nutrition

There are lots of different types of baby plants and vegetables that are eaten in their sprouting stage and are a powerhouse of nutrients. They're jam-packed full of vitamins, minerals, antioxidants, protein and enzymes that all have huge benefits to our health and wellbeing. When a plant or vegetable seed is germinated, its nutritional benefit increases anywhere between 300 and 1,200 per cent! So sprouted seeds are a pretty impressive condensed form of nutrients that shouldn't be ignored. A little goes a long way in the world of sprouts so a mere handful of these 'living foods' included in your diet can give you a really healthy boost and leave you bursting with energy. What's more, they can replace important enzymes in our bodies that we can no longer produce ourselves, as we get older.

where to find them

When it comes to sourcing sprouts, they are becoming increasingly more available in supermarkets, grocery stores and, of course, health food shops, which is great news. However, your best option of getting to enjoy a variety of sprouts regularly is to grow your own — and it's far easier than you might imagine.

how to sprout

You can buy all sorts of fancy sprouting seed trays and kits, but to get you started it can be as simple as using a fairly big screw-top jar (about 1–2l/35–70fl oz/4–8½ cups) and a lid with holes pierced into the top or a piece of muslin/cheesecloth securely attached to the top with a rubber band, for ventilation and drainage. I use a large Mason jar with a two-piece screw-top lid, replacing the metal disc with a piece of muslin/cheesecloth.

Details vary from seed to seed, but once you have some seeds or beans suitable for home sprouting (not planting) the general method is the same. Put the seeds into your clean jar (fill no more than one-third full). Rinse with cold water, drain and then top up with fresh cold water. Leave to soak overnight (or less if the seed/grain package says so). Rinse thoroughly, drain well (tip the jar upside down) and leave the jar on its side at room temperature, out of direct sunlight. Rinse and drain a couple of times a day (I find at breakfast time and before bed is the most practical time for me) and after 3–5 days you should have fully sprouted seeds. Make sure they are well drained, then keep in the refrigerator for up to 3 days.

flavours

Like vegetables, each and every type of sprout has a different flavour. These are just some of the types of sprouts around:

» Fresh and delicate microgreens - the baby leaves of vegetables such as beets, pea, rocket/arugula, clover and cress. These are very mild in flavour and can really enhance the presentation of a dish when scattered over the top.
» Spicy and add bite — radish, onion, fenugreek, garlic, mustard.
» Nutty and wholesome — these will add texture and crunch to a dish: mung beans, lentils, chickpeas, aduki, alfalfa and split peas.

what to make

As well as my recipe for Beef Carpaccio with Rocket and Alfalfa Salad (see page 56), here are a few suggestions on how to include some sprouts in your diet:

» Add to tossed salads or make them the star of a salad (mixture of any sprouts)
» Mix into coleslaw (cabbage, radish or clover)
» Scatter into wraps or sandwiches (alfalfa, sunflower, radish)
» Add to stir-fries (mung beans, aduki, lentil, cabbage)
» Add to sushi (radish, clover, sunflower, broccoli)
» Stir into soups, casseroles and stews (chickpea, mung bean, aduki, lentil)
» Mix into curries (chickpeas, fenugreek, lentils, mung bean, aduki)
» Blend into juices (broccoli, clover, alfalfa, pea shoots)
» Blend into hummus (chickpea)
» Garnish dishes (microgreens, alfalfa, onion, pea shoots)

vietnamese beef skewers with pickled carrot salad

600g/1lb 5oz sirloin steak (or 4 steaks, about 150g/5½oz each)
1 lemongrass stalk, finely chopped
2 garlic cloves, crushed
2 spring onions/scallions, finely chopped
4 tbsp fish sauce
2 tbsp palm sugar or soft brown sugar

For the pickled carrot salad:
125ml/4fl oz/½ cup white wine vinegar
2 tbsp palm sugar or soft brown sugar
1 red bird's eye chilli, finely chopped
4 large carrots, peeled
1 red onion, very finely sliced
1 handful of coriander/cilantro leaves

Munching on raw carrots is a very healthy thing to do – after all they are packed with vitamin A – but quite frankly, that isn't everyone's idea of fun! So, why not make the humble carrot a little more interesting and pickle it. This is a quick pickling recipe so the nutrients are not all lost in the process by cooking them away. Served with super-tasty beef skewers, you'll want to make this recipe over and over again. Before you know it, you might find you really can see in the dark.

Trim away any fat from the steak and thinly slice into long strips. Put in a bowl and combine with the lemongrass, garlic, spring onions/scallions, fish sauce and sugar. Cover and leave to marinate in the refrigerator for a minimum of 20–30 minutes. Overnight is fine if you have time.

Meanwhile, to make the salad, put the white wine vinegar, sugar and chilli in a small saucepan and bring to the boil over a medium-high heat, stirring until the sugar dissolves. Remove from the heat and transfer to a large non-reactive bowl to cool.

Slice the carrots into matchsticks, ideally using a julienne peeler or mandoline. If you don't have either, cut as thinly as you can into long sticks with a sharp knife. Add to the bowl of cooled vinegar with the red onion. Mix well and leave to one side to allow the carrot to 'pickle' for about 30 minutes.

To cook the beef, thread a few strips onto each metal skewer in a rippled effect. Heat a griddle/grill pan over a high heat until smoking hot. Cook the skewers for about 3–4 minutes on each side, or until just cooked through and deep golden on the outside. Serve with the pickled carrot and scatter with coriander/cilantro leaves.

pea and crab soup

SERVES 4

preparation time: 10 minutes, plus 10 minutes cooling

cooking time: 15 minutes

2 tbsp olive oil

1 onion, sliced

2 garlic cloves, crushed

2 strips of peeled lemon zest

1 bay leaf

600ml/21fl oz/2½ cups fish stock

400g/14oz/2⅔ cups frozen peas

75g/2½oz parsley leaves and stalks, roughly chopped

100–150g/3½–5½oz white and brown crab meat (a half-and-half mix is perfect)

a squeeze of lemon juice

sea salt

extra virgin olive oil, for drizzling

cayenne pepper, to serve

I love making pea soup, mainly because it's so quick to make, uses very few basic ingredients and yet tastes amazing. Peas are really good for you as they are high in vitamin C, but to make this soup even healthier I've added a rather large amount of parsley. A common herb that often gets taken for granted, it is in fact very high in essential oils that are great for your kidneys (and known to be cancer protective) and a great source of folate (a very important nutrient for women who are looking to conceive). Pea and parsley soup is a great everyday soup to make, but to push the dish one step further, the addition of crab makes it a little bit special. You'll be adding protein and omega-3 fatty acids and a lovely flavour, too. It's subtle and delicate, perfect for entertaining when you want a healthy (and easy) start to your meal.

Heat the olive oil in a saucepan over a medium heat and sauté the onion for about 5 minutes until softened but not coloured. Stir in the garlic, lemon zest and bay leaf and cook for a further 2 minutes. Add the stock and bring to the boil, then add the peas and parsley. Return to the boil and cook for 3 minutes.

Remove from the heat and leave to cool for about 10 minutes before removing the lemon and bay leaf and blitzing the soup in a food processor or blender until it is smooth. (Leaving it to cool will make blitzing it easier. If it's too hot, the steam can make the lid come off and you lose the soup – I've learnt this the hard way.)

Return the soup to the saucepan, stir in the crab meat and gently heat through. Season to taste with a squeeze of lemon juice and salt, and ladle into bowls. Serve drizzled with extra virgin olive oil and a little cayenne pepper.

5-spice prawn ramen

SERVES 4

preparation time: 20 minutes

cooking time: 15 minutes

300g/10½oz large raw, peeled prawns/shrimp

2 tsp Chinese 5 spice

1 tbsp toasted sesame oil, plus extra for the noodles

½ tsp salt

½ tsp caster/granulated sugar

350g/12oz ramen or udon noodles

1.5l/52fl oz/6¼ cups vegetable stock

75g/2½oz shiitake mushrooms, thinly sliced

2 garlic cloves, thinly sliced

2.5cm/1in piece of root ginger, peeled and cut into matchsticks

1 tbsp soy sauce, plus extra to serve

2 pak choi/bok choy, ends trimmed and cut in half

100g/3½oz/1¾ cups bean sprouts

75g/2½oz/⅔ cup sliced bamboo shoots

To serve:

4 spring onions/ scallions, finely sliced diagonally

1 red chilli, finely sliced

1 small handful of coriander/cilantro

1 lime, cut into quarters

Ramen is a Japanese noodle soup that consists of stock and noodles, and is flavoured with soy or miso. It can have many different toppings, such as cooked sliced pork or chicken, vegetables and chillies. It's super-healthy and my recipe is packed full of fresh veg (more than a traditional ramen) and super-tasty prawns coated with 5-spice seasoning. Ok, so the ingredients list looks rather long, but seriously, it is all good stuff and the recipe itself is very easy to make. Once you've made this once, I'm sure you'll get carried away and will start to try out other combinations that take your fancy.

Toss together the prawns/shrimp, 5-spice, sesame oil, salt and sugar in a bowl and leave to one aside.

Cook the noodles according to the packet instructions (this should take about 5 minutes), then drain and toss in a little sesame oil to prevent them from sticking.

Meanwhile, put the stock, shiitake mushrooms, garlic, ginger and soy sauce in a large saucepan set over a medium heat and gently simmer for 5 minutes.

Heat a griddle/grill pan or frying pan over a high heat until hot. Cook the prawns/shrimp for about 1 minute on each side until they turn pink and golden.

Divide the cooked noodles, pak choi/bok choy, bean sprouts and bamboo shoots evenly into deep bowls. Spoon over the hot stock and divide the prawns/shrimp evenly among the bowls. Scatter with the spring onions/ scallions, chilli, a few stalks of coriander/cilantro and a wedge of lime. Serve with extra soy sauce to taste.

smoked salmon, samphire and asparagus salad

200g/7oz samphire

200g/7oz asparagus
  spears

200g/7oz smoked
  salmon, cut or torn
  into strips

1 ripe avocado, peeled,
  pitted and sliced into
  bite-size pieces

100g/3½oz/⅔ cup
  frozen peas, defrosted

1 small bunch of chives,
  about 10g/⅓oz, cut
  into 2.5cm/1in lengths

For the pink grapefruit dressing:

1 pink grapefruit

2 tbsp avocado or
  rapeseed/canola oil

1 tbsp honey

1 tsp white wine vinegar

1 tsp Dijon mustard

sea salt and freshly
  ground black pepper

If you've not cooked samphire before, now is your chance. It's a vibrant green sea vegetable, sometimes referred to as sea asparagus, that grows on shorelines. It has a fabulous crisp texture and salty taste, making it a perfect partner for fish. It's bursting with all sorts of nutrients for good health and teamed with asparagus, smoked salmon, avocado and peas you quite simply have a salad that's impressive enough for the poshest of dinner parties.

First, make the dressing. Cut the top and bottom off the grapefruit, then put it flat on a board. Following the curve of the fruit, cut away the peel and pith using a sharp knife. Hold the grapefruit over a bowl to catch the juices and cut out the segments, leaving behind the membrane between them. Cut each segment in half.

In a separate bowl, mix together the avocado oil, honey, white wine vinegar and mustard, and season with salt and pepper. Add the grapefruit segments and 1 tablespoon of the grapefruit juice. Gently mix and leave to one side.

Bring a pan of water to the boil. Trim the woody ends off the samphire and asparagus, then slice each asparagus spear in half lengthways. Blanch the samphire and asparagus for just 1 minute, then refresh in a bowl of iced water. Drain well and pat dry.

Put the samphire and asparagus into a serving bowl and add the salmon, avocado, peas and chives. Pour over the dressing, gently toss to combine and serve.

PS... If you can't find samphire, you can still try this. Simply double up on the asparagus quantity, or replace the samphire with fine green beans, blanching them with the asparagus.

seared tuna and watermelon salad

500g/1lb 2oz watermelon

½ cucumber

½ red onion, very thinly
   sliced

1 small bunch of dill,
   fronds roughly chopped

2 tbsp pumpkin seeds

4 tuna steaks, about
   100–150g/3½–5½oz
   each

olive oil, for rubbing

100g/3½oz/scant 1 cup
   crumbled feta cheese

sea salt and freshly
   ground black pepper

For the pomegranate dressing:

½ red chilli, finely
   chopped

1 tbsp pomegranate
   molasses

1 tbsp lemon juice

3 tbsp extra virgin olive
   oil

Fresh tuna is a truly fantastic healthy ingredient to eat for the amount of omega-3 fatty acids it contains, which can lower your cholesterol, reduce high blood pressure, protect you from heart attacks, reduce inflammation, fight wrinkles and improve your memory. We should all be eating more omega-3 rich foods and this is a great summery recipe to have a go at.

Cut the watermelon away from the skin. Slice the flesh into bite-size chunks and put in a large bowl, removing any pips that come out easily.

Peel and halve the cucumber and remove the seeds. Cut into slightly smaller chunks than the watermelon and add to the bowl, along with the sliced red onion and chopped dill.

Heat a non-stick frying pan over a medium-high heat and dry-fry the pumpkin seeds for 2–3 minutes, or until they start to puff slightly and turn lightly golden. Remove from the pan and leave to cool.

Heat a frying pan or griddle/grill pan until smoking hot. Rub the tuna steaks in a little olive oil and season with salt and pepper. Add the tuna to the pan and sear for about 1 minute on each side until browned but still pink inside. Remove from the pan and leave to rest for a few minutes. If you prefer your tuna well done just increase the cooking time slightly, but do keep in mind that it will continue to cook as it rests.

To make the dressing, mix together the chilli, pomegranate molasses, lemon juice and extra virgin olive oil in a small bowl. Season with salt and pepper. Pour over the salad and gently toss everything together. Spoon onto plates and scatter over the pumpkin seeds and crumbled feta.

Slice each tuna steak into three pieces, then serve the salad topped with the tuna.

SERVES 4

preparation time: 15 minutes
cooking time: 20 minutes

smoked trout and beetroot frittata with avocado salsa

2 tbsp rapeseed/canola
    oil
1 onion, finely sliced
120g/4¼oz cooked
    beetroot/beets, cut into
    1cm/½in cubes
100g/3½oz smoked trout
    fillet, flaked
1 large handful of dill,
    chopped
5 eggs, lightly beaten
sea salt and freshly
    ground black pepper

For the avocado salsa:
2 tbsp pumpkin seeds
1 avocado, peeled, pitted
    and cut into small
    chunks
3 spring onions/
    scallions, finely sliced
1 celery stalk, finely diced
1 tbsp lemon juice
1 tbsp rapeseed/canola oil
1 large handful of
    sprouting seeds or tub
    of salad cress

Not only is this one of the most colourful of dishes, it's also packed full of good stuff from start to finish. I agree that beetroot/beets might not be an obvious choice to include in a frittata, but it tastes seriously good especially when combined with the smoked trout and generous amount of dill. Please don't skip the salsa – it rounds everything off just perfectly, not to mention adding even more goodness along the way.

Preheat the grill/broiler to high. Heat a non-stick frying pan over a medium-high heat and dry-fry the pumpkin seeds for 2–3 minutes, or until they start to puff slightly and turn lightly golden. Tip into a bowl and leave to cool.

To make the frittata, return the pan to the heat and add the rapeseed/canola oil. Fry the onion over a medium heat for about 8 minutes, or until softened and lightly golden. Stir in the beetroot/beets and fry for a couple of minutes to heat through.

Mix the trout and dill into the beaten eggs and season with salt and plenty of pepper. Pour into the frying pan with the onion and beetroot/beets and stir around with a rubber spatula until the eggs start to resemble very softly set scrambled egg. Level the surface and cook for 1–2 minutes until the base is set, then transfer to the grill/broiler and cook for about 4 minutes, or until the egg is just set.

Meanwhile, mix the remaining salsa ingredients into the pumpkin seeds and season with salt and pepper. Cut the cooked frittata into wedges and serve with the salsa.

✳ WASTE NOT, WANT NOT

Don't let the rest of your celery wither at the bottom of the refrigerator. Turn it into an amazingly tasty stir-fry with chilli and soy. Cut the celery into slim finger-length sticks. Heat a wok with a splash of toasted sesame oil. Add the celery and stir-fry for about 3 minutes. Throw in some finely chopped red chilli (as much or little as you wish) and a splash of dark soy sauce. Serve as it is or scattered with toasted sesame or black sesame seeds.

preparation time: 15 minutes
cooking time: 25 minutes

spiced lentil and sweet potato soup

a pinch of saffron strands

1 tbsp milk

½ tsp dried chilli/hot
  pepper flakes

2 tsp cumin seeds

2 tbsp olive oil

750g/1lb 10oz sweet
  potatoes, peeled and
  cut into small chunks

1 celery stalk, finely sliced

150g/5½oz/⅔ cup red
  lentils

1.2l/40fl oz/5 cups hot
  vegetable stock

200ml/7fl oz/scant 1 cup
  low-fat coconut milk

4 tbsp low-fat plain
  yogurt

sea salt and freshly
  ground black pepper

1 small handful of
  coriander/cilantro
  leaves, to serve

This is one of those soups that you should try and make when you've a spare half an hour or so to spend in the kitchen. Once made, the soup will keep in the refrigerator for up to one week or even better popped into the freezer in individual portions. You'll be so glad of it when all you want is an instant, comforting and healthy lunch. The star ingredient in this soup is the lentils. They're high in soluble fibre, which is great for lowering cholesterol, plus they add a good proportion of low-fat protein to your meal. The saffron yogurt isn't essential, but it certainly gives a fragrant finishing touch.

Mix the saffron with the milk in a small bowl and leave to one side.

Heat a large saucepan over a medium-low heat and add the chilli/hot pepper flakes and cumin seeds. Dry-fry for a minute or so until they release their aroma and pop around in the pan. Remove half of the seeds from the pan and leave to one side.

Add the oil to the pan and, when it is hot, stir in the sweet potatoes and celery. Cook for 5 minutes, stirring occasionally, then add the lentils, stock and coconut milk. Increase the heat to medium and bring to a simmer, then cover with a lid and cook for about 15 minutes, until the lentils are tender.

Blitz the soup with a hand-held/immersion blender until it is as smooth or chunky as you like, then season with salt and pepper.

Mix the saffron and milk with the yogurt and season with a pinch of salt.

Ladle the soup into bowls and swirl spoonfuls of the saffron yogurt on top. Scatter with the reserved toasted spices and a few coriander/cilantro leaves and serve.

souper green soup with pumpkin seed croutons

This is packed with green vegetable goodness, vitamins and minerals galore. The soup alone is great, but the croutons are a real tasty treat to scatter over the top. Salty, crunchy and very moreish.

2 tbsp olive oil

1 fennel bulb, finely chopped

4 garlic cloves, crushed

1 leek, thinly sliced

1 medium-large courgette/zucchini, sliced

1l/35fl oz/4 cups vegetable stock

300g/10½oz spring/ collard greens, roughly chopped

100g/3½oz/⅔ cup frozen peas, defrosted

1 large handful of mint leaves

sea salt and freshly ground black pepper

For the croutons:

100g/3½oz feta cheese

50g/1¾oz/⅔ cup pumpkin seeds

1 tbsp olive oil

¼ tsp dried chilli/hot pepper flakes

1 tsp sumac

Preheat the oven to 220°C/425°F/gas 7. Break the feta into small chunks and gently mix together with the pumpkin seeds, olive oil, dried chilli/hot pepper flakes and sumac. Spread in a single layer on a non-stick baking sheet and bake for 10–12 minutes, shaking the baking sheet once during cooking, to ensure even cooking. When cooked, the feta should be starting to turn golden in places and the pumpkin seeds will be crunchy and puffed up. Remove from the oven and leave to one side.

Meanwhile, make the soup. Heat the olive oil in a saucepan over a medium-low heat. Add the fennel and garlic and gently sauté for about 5 minutes until the fennel is softened but not coloured. Stir in the leek and courgette/zucchini and continue to sauté for 5 minutes, then add the stock. Increase the heat to medium and bring to a simmer, then add the spring/ collard greens and cook for 3 minutes. Stir in the peas, and as soon as the soup returns to a simmer, cook for 2 minutes. Remove the pan from the heat and add the mint.

Using a hand-held stick/immersion blender or electric blender, blitz the soup until it is smooth. Season with salt and pepper to taste and serve with the pumpkin seed and feta croutons scattered on top.

roast squash and garlic soup

SERVES 4

preparation time: 20 minutes, plus 10 minutes cooling

cooking time: 55 minutes

1 medium-large butternut squash, peeled

2 carrots, peeled

2 onions

olive oil, for drizzling

2 bulbs of garlic, left whole

1.3l/45fl oz/5½ cups vegetable stock, plus extra if needed

1 tsp dried chilli/hot pepper flakes

1½ tsp nigella seeds

1½ tsp fennel seeds

sea salt and freshly ground black pepper

Tuck into a bowlful of this hearty soup and you'll be safe forever from vampires! Garlic is such a brilliant everyday ingredient that is known for it's immune-strengthening, anti-inflammatory and anti-cancer properties. When roasted it takes on a rich, sweet, mellow flavour that blends so well with the roasted squash.

Heat the oven to 200°C/400°F/gas 6. Cut the squash, carrots and onions into chunky wedges. Put in a large roasting pan and drizzle with olive oil. Turn to coat everything in the oil and season with salt and pepper.

Wrap the garlic bulbs in separate pieces of foil. Put both the garlic and the roasting pan in the oven for about 45–50 minutes, turning the vegetables a couple of times during cooking, until they are cooked through and just turning golden. Remove the vegetables and garlic from the oven and leave to cool for about 10 minutes.

As soon as it is cool enough to handle, squeeze the roasted garlic out of the skins, straight into a blender. Add some of the roasted vegetables and some stock. Blend until really smooth. Transfer to a saucepan, and repeat with the remaining roasted vegetables and stock. Add any extra stock or water if the soup is too thick, until you reach a consistency you are happy with.

Gently heat the soup over a low heat and season with salt and pepper to taste. Crush the dried chilli/hot pepper flakes and nigella and fennel seeds in a pestle and mortar. Ladle the soup into bowls and sprinkle a little of the crushed seeds over to serve, offering any extra separately.

preparation time: 15 minutes
cooking time: 30 minutes

carrot, ginger and apple soup

2 tbsp olive or rapeseed/
   canola oil
1 onion, chopped
750g/1lb 10oz carrots,
   peeled and sliced
1 Bramley apple, peeled,
   cored and roughly
   chopped
2 garlic cloves, crushed
5cm/2in piece of root
   ginger, peeled and
   chopped
1 bay leaf
1l/35fl oz/4 cups
   vegetable stock
sea salt and freshly
   ground black pepper

Simplicity at its best. This nourishing soup has a really nice sweet, tangy flavour from the apple and carrot, and the root ginger adds a subtle warmth. It can be served either hot or as a chilled soup in the summer months.

Heat the oil in a large saucepan over a medium heat and gently sauté the onion for about 5 minutes until softened but not coloured. Add the carrots, apple, garlic, ginger and bay leaf. Cover with a lid and cook for 5 minutes, stirring a couple of times to prevent anything from sticking or colouring in the base of the pan. (The steam being created in the pan should also prevent this.)

Pour in the stock, bring to a simmer and loosely cover with a lid. Cook for 20 minutes, or until the carrots are tender.

Remove the bay leaf from the soup and, using a hand-held/immersion blender or electric blender, blitz the soup until it is smooth. Season with salt and pepper to taste and serve hot or chilled.

preparation time: 20 minutes
cooking time: 55 minutes

winter vegetable broth with zesty parsley dressing

2 tbsp rapeseed/canola
  oil
1 leek, sliced
2 celery stalks, finely
  sliced
2 carrots, peeled and cut
  into 1–2cm/½–¾in
  dice
1 parsnip, peeled and cut
  into 1–2cm/½–¾in
  dice
½ small swede/rutabaga,
  peeled and cut into
  1–2cm/½–¾in dice
2 bay leaves
2 thyme stalks
100g/3½oz/½ cup pearl
  barley
80ml/2½fl oz/⅓ cup
  white wine
1.2l/40fl oz/5 cups
  vegetable or chicken
  stock
1 tbsp tomato purée/paste
sea salt and freshly
  ground black pepper

For the zesty parsley dressing:
1 large bunch of parsley
4 tbsp olive oil
zest of 1 lemon
3 tbsp lemon juice
1 tsp sugar

This wholesome broth is given an even healthier boost with the vibrant green parsley dressing. Parsley is known to be great for supporting kidney functions not to mention being rich in numerous vital vitamins – so pretty good stuff indeed. Feel free to use other veg that you might have in your refrigerator for this recipe and you can also swap fibre-rich pearl barley with pearled spelt or farro, if you have some.

To make the broth, heat the rapeseed/canola oil in a large saucepan and add all of the vegetables. Cook over a medium heat for about 5 minutes until the vegetables just start to soften.

Stir in the bay leaves, thyme, pearl barley, white wine, stock and tomato purée/paste. Bring to a simmer, then cook for about 45 minutes until the vegetables are very tender and the pearl barley is soft.

Meanwhile, blitz together all of the parsley dressing ingredients in a food processor or blender. Add a little water to loosen to a thick pouring consistency. Season with salt and pepper and leave to one side.

Remove the bay leaves and thyme stalks from the broth and season with salt and pepper. Ladle into bowls, spoon or drizzle the parsley dressing over the top and serve.

japanese miso, kale and tofu broth

1.5l/52fl oz/6¼ cups chicken or vegetable stock

6 tbsp white miso paste

2 garlic cloves, crushed

2.5cm/1in piece of root ginger, peeled and grated

1 red chilli, finely sliced

4 spring onions/ scallions, finely sliced

100g/3½oz/3 cups trimmed and shredded kale

175g/6oz firm tofu, drained and cut into 1cm/½in cubes

1½ tbsp rice vinegar

Oh my goodness. This just has to be one of the easiest of broths to make and the sheer satisfaction you get when you've slurped a bowlful of this is amazing. It's cleansing, filling, nourishing, comforting and refreshing, and I can't get enough of it. If you haven't any kale, you can use any greens you like for this; cavolo nero, cabbage, spring/collard greens, chard or even spinach, depending on the time of year.

Bring the stock to the boil in a large saucepan set over a high heat, then add the miso paste, garlic, ginger and chilli. Stir until the miso has dissolved and leave to simmer gently over a medium heat for 5 minutes.

Stir in the spring onions/scallions, kale, tofu and rice vinegar. Cook gently for 4–5 minutes until the kale is just tender. Ladle into bowls and serve.

*WASTE NOT, WANT NOT

Miso paste is great for using in marinades, soups and dressings. One of my favourite ways to use up miso is to make an Asian Coleslaw. Whisk together 80ml/2½fl oz/ ⅓ cup rice vinegar with 3 tablespoons miso paste, 2 teaspoons soft brown sugar, 2 teaspoons finely grated root ginger, 2 teaspoons toasted sesame oil, 2 teaspoons soy sauce, 3 tablespoons olive oil and 4 tablespoons plain yogurt. Toss into plenty of finely shredded veggies, such as mange tout/snow peas, sugar snap peas, cabbage, spinach, spring onions/scallions and carrots.

preparation time: 10 minutes, plus at least 30 minutes chilling

raw mexican gazpacho soup

800g/1lb 12oz very ripe plum tomatoes, quartered

½ red onion, roughly chopped

¾ cucumber, roughly chopped

1 red pepper, deseeded and quartered

1 yellow pepper, deseeded and quartered

1 green chilli, roughly chopped

2 garlic cloves, crushed

4 tbsp extra virgin olive oil, plus extra for drizzling

3 tbsp lime juice

1 small handful of coriander/cilantro leaves

1 large ripe avocado

sea salt and freshly ground black pepper

I've given my favourite chilled soup, Spanish gazpacho, a wave of Mexican flavours by adding lime, green chilli, mixed peppers and coriander/cilantro to the original recipe. It all works wonderfully well together and is a fabulously quick, not to mention, healthy soup to serve during the summer months with vitamins and minerals galore in their raw form. To take the Mexican idea further, I like to serve the soup with omega-rich diced avocado on top and crisp tortilla 'croutons'.

Put the tomatoes, onion, cucumber, red and yellow peppers, chilli, garlic, olive oil, 2 tablespoons of the lime juice and the coriander/cilantro (reserving some to serve) in a blender or food processor and whizz until smooth. Season with salt and pepper, then chill for at least 30 minutes.

Just before serving, peel the avocado, remove the pit and cut into 1cm/½in dice. Mix with the remaining 1 tablespoon of lime juice and season with salt and pepper.

Ladle the chilled soup into bowls or cups. Spoon a little of the avocado mixture on top and drizzle with a little olive oil. Add a twist of pepper and scatter over the reserved coriander/cilantro leaves.

Serve the soup with tortilla croutons (see below), if you like.

*HOW TO MAKE: TORTILLA 'CROUTONS'

Here's a tasty little accompaniment if you fancy it with the soup. Heat the oven to 200°C/400°F/gas 6. Brush a little olive oil over both sides of wheat-flour or corn tortillas. Sprinkle with salt and a dusting of smoked paprika. Cut into triangles or strips and put on a baking sheet. Bake for 6–8 minutes until golden and crispy. Once made, they will keep for up to 1 week in an airtight container.

preparation time: 20 minutes,
plus cooling
cooking time: 30 minutes

roast carrot and feta salad with tahini dressing

1kg/2lb 4oz carrots,
   peeled and cut into
   thick batons
3 tbsp olive oil
1 tsp ground cumin
½ tsp cayenne pepper
1 tbsp honey
400g/14oz canned
   chickpeas, drained
75g/2½oz/1½ cups
   spinach, watercress or
   rocket/arugula leaves
seeds from 1 large
   pomegranate, or 150g/
   5½oz ready-prepared
   pomegranate seeds
150g/5½oz feta cheese
2 tbsp toasted pumpkin
   seeds or roughly
   chopped pistachio nuts
sea salt and freshly
   ground black pepper

For the tahini dressing:
2 tbsp tahini
juice of 1 lemon
2 tbsp extra virgin olive
   oil
1 small garlic clove,
   crushed

Carrots feature quite a few times in this book, and all for good reason. They are rich in vitamins C and E, calcium, beta-carotene (which converts to vitamin A), magnesium and potassium, all of which benefit your body by cleansing your liver, encouraging detoxing and protecting your vision against degenerative conditions. I never tire of this salad — it has a vibrant colour, mouthwatering flavours and is far more substantial than a plateful of salad leaves. Serve as a sharing platter for four or as a main for two.

Preheat the oven to 190°C/375°F/gas 5. Put the carrots in a roasting pan and toss together with the olive oil, cumin and cayenne pepper and season with salt. Roast for 20 minutes, turning a couple of times during cooking.

Drizzle the honey over the carrots and toss to coat. Stir in the chickpeas and return to the oven for a further 10 minutes until the carrots are tender and turning golden. Leave to cool to room temperature.

To make the dressing, mix together all the ingredients in a small bowl and add a little water to give a looser pouring consistency, if necessary. Season with salt and pepper.

Toss the cooled roasted carrots and chickpeas with the salad leaves, pomegranate seeds and feta cheese. Spoon onto a large serving dish or individual plates and drizzle over the dressing. Serve scattered with pumpkin seeds.

⁎ WASTE NOT, WANT NOT

Any leftover feta cheese can be used to make the (very moreish) croutons on page 76. Use to sprinkle on top of soups and salads, or nibble them throughout the day.

cauliflower couscous with pine nuts and chickpeas

1 cauliflower

1 tbsp olive oil

75g/2½oz/scant ½ cup
  pine nuts

75g/2½oz/½ cup
  raisins

½ tsp ground
  coriander

½ tsp ground cumin

¼ tsp ground turmeric

a pinch of dried chilli/
  hot pepper flakes

400g/14oz canned
  chickpeas, drained

finely grated zest of
  1 lemon

1 large handful of
  parsley, chopped

4 spring onions/
  scallions, finely sliced

sea salt

Get ready to blow the minds of whoever you are serving this salad to as they will be very surprised to hear that the couscous they are eating isn't couscous at all. It is in fact raw cauliflower blitzed in a food processor to resemble the texture of couscous. It's genius – and of course low-carb, high in nutrients and an excellent source of antioxidants, not to mention being ridiculously quick to make.

Cut the cauliflower into quarters and remove the core. Put half of the cauliflower in a food processor and pulse until it resembles couscous. Be careful not to over-blitz at this stage. Transfer to a bowl and repeat with the remaining cauliflower.

Heat a large frying pan over a medium heat and add the oil. Add the pine nuts, raisins and dried spices and chilli/hot pepper flakes. Cook for about 2 minutes, stirring continuously, until the pine nuts are golden. Toss in the chickpeas and fry until heated through.

Add the cauliflower 'couscous' and a good pinch of salt. Toss and move around in the pan over a high heat for 3–4 minutes to very lightly cook the cauliflower.

Transfer to a large bowl and stir through the lemon zest, parsley and spring onions/scallions. Serve hot or cold.

warm goats' cheese, blueberry and walnut salad

300–400g/10½–14oz
 goats' cheese log with
 rind on, or 4 individual
 rounds
a few thyme sprigs
50g/1¾oz/heaped ½ cup
 dried breadcrumbs
2 tbsp olive oil, plus extra
 for brushing
100g/3½oz mixed baby
 salad leaves
1 large ripe avocado,
 peeled, pitted and diced
200g/7oz/1½ cups
 blueberries

For the crunchy walnuts:
100g/3½oz/1 cup walnut
 halves
1 tbsp olive oil
2 tsp sugar
¼ tsp hot chilli powder

For the walnut dressing:
3 tbsp walnut oil
1 tbsp red wine vinegar
2 tsp honey
1 tsp Dijon mustard
sea salt and freshly
 ground black pepper

It might not be your first choice of fruit to add to a veggie salad – but juicy, not-too-sweet blueberries work really well when teamed with creamy goats' cheese and sweet crunchy walnuts. They are wonderfully high in antioxidants – one of the highest among all fruits – and thought to protect against heart disease and cholesterol.

Preheat the oven to 180°C/350°F/gas 4 and line a baking sheet with baking parchment. Toss the walnuts with the olive oil, sugar, chilli powder and a pinch of salt. Spread them onto the prepared baking sheet and bake for 10–15 minutes, turning occasionally, until crunchy. Leave to cool.

To make the walnut dressing, whisk all of the ingredients together in a small bowl or shake together in a small jar. Season with salt and pepper.

If you are using a large log of goats' cheese, slice the rind off the ends if there is any there, and cut the log into 4 individual rounds. If you are using individual rounds, make sure there is only rind on the outer edges, slicing off any rind from the flat surface.

Remove the leaves from the thyme sprigs and finely chop them. Mix together with the breadcrumbs in a shallow dish and season with pepper. Brush both flat sides of the goats' cheese rounds with a little olive oil, then press into the breadcrumbs, lightly coating both sides.

Heat the olive oil in a frying pan over a medium heat. Fry the crumbed goats' cheese rounds for a couple of minutes on each side until they are lightly golden.

Meanwhile, divide the salad leaves and avocado evenly onto plates. Top with the goats' cheese, then scatter over the blueberries and crunchy walnuts. Drizzle with the dressing and serve.

preparation time: 15 minutes, plus cooling

cooking time: 1¾–2¼ hours

herby chickpea tabbouleh with oven-dried tomatoes

12 smallish (about the size of a golf ball) ripe tomatoes, halved lengthways

125g/4½oz/¾ cup bulgur wheat

400g/14oz canned chickpeas, drained

1 bunch of flat leaf parsley, roughly chopped

1 bunch of mint, roughly chopped

1 bunch of spring onions/ scallions, finely sliced

seeds from 1 pomegranate, or 100g/3½oz ready-prepared pomegranate seeds

3 tbsp extra virgin olive oil

juice and finely grated zest of 1 lemon

200g/7oz feta cheese, broken into small pieces

sea salt and freshly ground black pepper

Traditionally, tabbouleh, a Middle Eastern parsley salad, contains very little bulgur wheat and is served as part of a mezze platter. However, here I've increased the bulgur wheat and added some chickpeas and feta, making this a more plentiful salad that is absolutely delicious, particularly during the summer. The oven-dried tomatoes give a rich sweetness to the finished dish. If you know you'll be short of time on the day you plan to make this recipe, the tomatoes can be made them a day or so ahead of time and stored in the refrigerator.

Preheat the oven to 130°C/250°F/gas 1. Put the tomatoes on a baking sheet, cut side up, and bake for 1½–2 hours. This is just enough time for the tomatoes to start to dry out and begin to shrivel around the edges, which will intensify their flavour and make them wonderfully sweet and juicy. Remove from the oven and leave to cool.

Cook the bulgur wheat according to the packet instructions, then cool under cold running water. Drain well, shaking the sieve/strainer to separate all the grains, then tip into a large mixing bowl.

Add the chickpeas, herbs, spring onions/scallions, pomegranate seeds, olive oil, lemon zest and juice to the bulgur wheat and season with salt and pepper.

Gently stir in the feta, then serve with the tomatoes.

*⁎ WASTE NOT, WANT NOT

While your oven is on, it is well worth making a job lot of the tomatoes so you've plenty to use on other days. They can be kept for up to 1 week in the refrigerator or for longer storage, put in a sterilized jar, cover with olive oil, seal and keep in a cool place. As long as the tomatoes are immersed in oil, they will keep for weeks. Use in pasta, salads and anti-pasti, or scatter over roast meat and fish dishes.

soft-boiled egg and barley salad

115g/4oz/½ cup pearl barley
750ml/26fl oz/3 cups chicken stock
1 garlic clove, peeled and halved
1 bay leaf
4 eggs, at room temperature
115g/4oz radishes, finely sliced
1 small bunch of flat leaf parsley, chopped
1 tub salad cress

For the honey and mustard dressing:
3 tbsp rapeseed/canola oil
2 tsp sherry vinegar
1 tsp wholegrain mustard
½ tsp honey
sea salt and freshly ground black pepper

Such simplicity, yet such amazing flavours. The peppery salad cress and radishes really make this dish. If you want to try a different grain, pearled spelt, farro or bulgur wheat would be delicious, but for me the nuttiness and bite from pearl barley is pretty special. I'll often serve this as a first course for four before a light main course, though it is certainly substantial enough to serve two as a main course.

Rinse the pearl barley and leave to soak for 10 minutes in a bowl of cold water. Drain and rinse well under cold running water. Transfer to a saucepan and add the stock, garlic and bay leaf. Bring to the boil over a high heat, then cover with a lid, reduce the heat to medium and cook for 30 minutes, or until the barley is tender. Drain the barley and discard the bay leaf and garlic. Leave to cool to room temperature.

Bring a small saucepan of water to the boil. Add the eggs and when the water returns to the boil, cook for 6 minutes. Remove the eggs from the pan and leave to cool slightly before carefully peeling off the shells.

To make the dressing, mix together all the ingredients in a bowl with a small whisk. Season with salt and pepper, then add the pearl barley, sliced radishes and chopped parsley.

Spoon the barley onto plates and scatter with the salad cress. Cut the eggs in half and divide among the plates. Add a pinch of salt and a twist of pepper, then serve.

fried sesame tofu with soba noodle salad

For the sesame tofu:

450g/1lb firm tofu

3 tbsp sesame seeds

1 tbsp cornflour/
   cornstarch

2 tsp Chinese 5-spice

½ tsp salt

¼ tsp dried chilli/hot
   pepper flakes

rapeseed/canola oil, for
   frying

For the soba noodle salad:

200g/7oz soba
   (buckwheat) noodles

1 large carrot, peeled and
   cut into matchsticks

⅓ cucumber, halved,
   deseeded and cut into
   matchsticks

100g/3½oz radishes,
   thinly sliced

4 spring onions/
   scallions, finely sliced
   diagonally

2 tbsp toasted sesame oil

2 tbsp soy sauce

4 tbsp rice vinegar

2 garlic cloves, crushed

2.5cm/1in piece of root
   ginger, peeled and
   grated

I have to admit, tofu wasn't ever really a favourite of mine, but I am aware of how healthy it is and it's a brilliant blank canvas that will absorb all sorts of flavour combinations. Powerful ones work the best, which is one of the reasons why it's used in many Asian dishes. This spicy sesame crust works brilliantly, giving a delicious full-flavoured crunch to the silky smooth tofu. For the salad, it's well worth getting hold of a serrated peeler as it will not only speed up cutting the carrot and cucumber into matchstick pieces, but also give you a far prettier end result.

Cook the noodles in a pan of boiling water according to the packet instructions. Drain well and refresh under cold running water. Put in a large mixing bowl and add the carrot, cucumber, radishes and spring onions/scallions.

In a separate bowl, mix together the sesame oil, soy sauce, rice vinegar, garlic and ginger. Pour over the noodle salad and toss together to combine, then leave to one side.

Drain the tofu and pat dry. Cut the block into 8 slices, 1cm/½in thick.

Combine the sesame seeds, cornflour/cornstarch, Chinese 5-spice, salt and chilli/hot pepper flakes on a plate. Press the tofu slices into the spice mix to evenly coat.

Heat 5mm/¼in rapeseed/canola oil in a frying pan over a medium-low heat. Cook the tofu slices for 2–3 minutes on each side (in batches, if necessary) until golden. Drain on paper towels and serve hot with the noodle salad.

avocado, carrot and cucumber temaki

150g/5½oz/heaped ¾ cup sushi rice

2 tbsp rice vinegar

1 tbsp caster/granulated sugar

6 sheets of sushi nori (seaweed), halved

2 ripe avocados, peeled, pitted and sliced into 12 strips

½ cucumber, deseeded and sliced into 12 sticks 5–6cm/2–2½in long

2 tubs salad or mustard cress

2 small-medium carrots, cut into julienne strips

1 tbsp toasted sesame seeds

sea salt

To serve:

Japanese pickled ginger

soy sauce

wasabi paste

Tucking into a plate of sushi is such a healthy way to eat, and making your own is far easier than you think. You'll get such a sense of achievement when you have done it, too. The first couple will be a case of trial and error and may not look very neat, but once you get the hang of it, they really are quite straightforward. These temaki are vegetarian and use a nice selection of fresh ingredients; however, you can be as adventurous as you wish, adding all sorts of seafood (just make sure it is really fresh, particularly raw fish) or even cooked meats.

To cook the sushi rice, rinse in cold running water until the water runs clear, then drain. Put into a medium saucepan with 150ml/5fl oz/scant ⅔ cup water. Cover with a lid and bring to the boil, then reduce the heat to medium, cover with a lid and leave to cook for 15 minutes. Turn off the heat and, without removing the lid, leave to stand for 10 minutes for the rice to finish cooking in the pan.

Meanwhile, gently heat the rice vinegar, sugar and a pinch of salt in a small saucepan until the sugar has dissolved.

Transfer the cooked rice to a bowl and pour over the rice vinegar mixture. Using a fork, stir into the rice, separating the grains and making sure they are all coated with the rice vinegar mixture. Leave to cool, stirring occasionally.

To make the temaki, put a strip of nori lengthways on the palm of your hand, shiny side down. Take a spoon of cool rice and put onto the bottom third of the nori strip.

Put some avocado, cucumber, cress, carrot and a sprinkle of sesame seeds on top of the rice widthways.

Fold the bottom-right corner of nori over towards the top left-hand corner of the rice, and continue to fold/roll into a cone shape, covering the rice and fillings with the nori. Secure by putting a piece of rice onto the last corner of nori and pressing to stick.

Repeat with the remaining ingredients to make 12 temaki, then serve with pickled ginger, soy sauce and wasabi.

tofu fritters with ponzu dipping sauce

200g/7oz silken tofu, drained

2 eggs

4 tbsp cornflour/ cornstarch

6 spring onions/ scallions, finely chopped

1 green chilli, finely chopped

olive or rapeseed/canola oil, for frying

sea salt

For the ponzu dipping sauce:

4 tbsp soy sauce

2 tbsp yuzu juice, or a combination of ¾ lime juice and ¼ orange juice

2 tbsp rice wine

2 tsp grated root ginger

If you think tofu isn't really your thing, then please do give these a try. It's very healthy as it's high in calcium, protein and iron, and doesn't contain any bad fats. These light, fluffy fritters are quite simply delicious and a breeze to make. The ponzu dipping sauce has a lovely salty, sweet and sour flavour with just the right amount of ginger to complement yet not overpower the otherwise delicate flavour of the fritters. Yuzu is an aromatic, Asian citrus fruit that is very high in vitamin C. Its juice, widely available in small bottles, is a classic ingredient used in ponzu dipping sauce.

To make the ponzu, simply mix everything together in a non-reactive bowl and leave to one side to allow the ginger to infuse.

Meanwhile, put the tofu in a mixing bowl and beat with a spoon or whisk until smooth. Add the eggs and mix, then stir in the cornflour/cornstarch, spring onions/scallions and chilli. Season with salt.

Preheat the oven to its lowest setting. Heat a large frying pan over a medium heat until hot, then add enough oil to just cover the base of the pan. Spoon tablespoons of the mixture into the pan, allowing space between for spreading. Cook for 2 minutes until the fritters start to set and dry out around the edges and the bases are golden. Carefully flip them over with a spatula and continue to cook for a further 2 minutes. Repeat until all the mixture is used up, keeping them warm in the oven while making the rest. You should make about 12 fritters.

Serve the fritters hot with the ponzu sauce for dipping.

baked root vegetable falafel with green yogurt

SERVES 4

preparation time: 25 minutes, plus 15 minutes cooling

cooking time: 55 minutes

1 large parsnip, peeled (about 200g/7oz peeled weight)

1 sweet potato, peeled (about 375g/13oz peeled weight)

½ butternut squash, peeled (about 600g/ 1lb 5oz peeled weight)

4 garlic cloves, unpeeled

4 tbsp olive oil

½ tsp ground cumin

½ tsp ground coriander

½ tsp hot chilli powder

3 tbsp sesame seeds

2 tbsp finely chopped parsley leaves

finely grated zest of 1 lemon

1 tsp salt

4–6 tbsp gram (chickpea) flour

flatbread and selection of mezze dishes, to serve

For the green yogurt:

185ml/6fl oz/¾ cup low-fat Greek yogurt

1 small bunch of coriander/cilantro, leaves and stalks

1 garlic clove, crushed

* *PS...* You could also stuff the falafel into a flatbread, drizzle the yogurt over the top and serve with a salad.

These are a great way to use up any root veggies you might have around, not to mention give you a good dose of fibre and numerous vitamins and minerals. I've used sweet potato, parsnip and butternut squash here, which is a tasty combination, though you could also use carrot, swede/rutabaga, turnip or other types of squash. Unlike traditional falafel, I bake these rather than deep-fry them, which is a much healthier way of cooking. They make a great first course with the green yogurt to dip into, or you can make a bigger meal of them with wholemeal/whole-wheat flatbread or pitta, baby spinach leaves, pickled chillies and juicy pomegranate seeds scattered over.

Preheat the oven to 200°C/400°F/gas 6. Remove the core from the parsnip if it seems tough and cut the peeled sweet potato, parsnip and butternut squash into 3cm/1¼in chunks. Put in a roasting pan with the garlic cloves and toss in half of the olive oil and dried spices. Cover with foil and roast for about 30 minutes until tender and just starting to take on some colour.

Transfer the vegetables to a bowl. Squeeze the soft roasted garlic out of the skins and add to the bowl. Mash well with a potato masher, then mix in the sesame seeds, parsley, lemon zest, salt and enough gram flour for the mixture to become sticky and be able to hold its shape when spooned out. Ideally, leave to cool for about 10–15 minutes before shaping.

If you have turned the oven off after baking the vegetables, preheat it again to 200°C/400°F/gas 6. Line a baking sheet with foil. Taking a spoonful at a time, roll the mixture into walnut-size balls with your hands and put on the prepared baking sheet. Drizzle the falafels with the remaining olive oil and roll around to coat. Bake for 20–25 minutes, turning a couple of times during cooking, until lightly golden.

To make the green yogurt, put all the ingredients in a food processor or blender and blitz until smooth. Spoon into a bowl and serve with the falafel for dipping, alongside flatbreads and other mezze dishes.

main meals

cajun chicken with beans and greens salad

SERVES 4

preparation time: 20 minutes, plus overnight soaking, marinating and cooling
cooking time: 30 minutes

1 tbsp olive oil
2 garlic cloves, crushed
1 tsp paprika
½ tsp cayenne pepper
1 tsp dried oregano
4 skinless, boneless chicken breast fillets
sea salt and freshly ground black pepper

For the beans and greens salad:
60g/2¼oz/⅓ cup dried mung beans, soaked in cold water overnight in the refrigerator
juice and zest of 1 lime
1 green chilli, deseeded and finely chopped
1 tbsp honey
3 tbsp olive oil
150g/5½oz slim stalks of broccoli, cut into small pieces
100g/3½oz green beans, halved
400g/14oz canned kidney beans, drained
400g/14oz canned black-eyed beans, drained
1 bunch of spring onions/ scallions, chopped
50g/1¾oz/1⅔ cups baby watercress, rocket/ arugula or baby spinach leaves
1 bunch of coriander/ cilantro, leaves chopped

They say that big things come in small packages and one of the ingredients in this recipe certainly lives up to the saying. Mung beans are said to defend against cancers, obesity, cardiovascular disease and diabetes – they also taste amazing when combined with spicy chicken, tangy lime and other types of bean. This is a recipe you'll turn to again and again for many reasons – it's the Swiss Army knife of everyday dishes.

To make the Cajun spice for the chicken, mix together the olive oil, garlic, paprika, cayenne pepper and oregano in a large mixing bowl. Add a good pinch of salt and some pepper.

Slash each chicken breast 3–4 times with a sharp knife. Add to the Cajun spices and mix thoroughly to coat the chicken in the spices. Cover and leave to marinate in the refrigerator for at least 30 minutes, or overnight if you want to prepare the chicken when you soak the mung beans.

Meanwhile, bring a saucepan of water to the boil over a medium-high heat and add the drained mung beans. Bring to a simmer, then reduce the heat to medium and cook for 10–15 minutes until just tender. Drain well and tip into a bowl. Mix in the lime juice, green chilli, honey and olive oil and leave to cool.

Lightly cook the broccoli and green beans by either steaming or boiling in water for 3–4 minutes until just tender. Add to the mung beans and toss to coat in the dressing. Leave to cool.

Heat a griddle/grill pan or frying pan over a medium heat. Add the chicken and cook for 4–5 minutes on each side until slightly charred and cooked through. Transfer to a plate and leave to rest.

Mix the canned beans, spring onions/scallions, salad leaves and coriander/ cilantro into the mung bean salad and toss together to coat everything in the dressing.

Cut the chicken in half or thirds diagonally, pour over any resting juices, scatter with lime zest and serve with the bean salad.

SERVES 4
preparation time: 10 minutes
cooking time: 15 minutes

chilli poached chicken with sesame soba noodles

4 lemongrass stalks

400ml/14fl oz/1⅔ cups chicken stock

2 tbsp fish sauce

70ml/2¼fl oz/generous ¼ cup lime juice

1 long red chilli, deseeded and finely sliced

2 fresh or dried kaffir lime leaves, finely shredded

2.5cm/1in piece of root ginger, peeled and cut into matchsticks

40g/1½oz/scant ¼ cup soft light brown sugar

4 skinless, boneless chicken breast fillets

300g/10½oz soba (buckwheat) noodles

toasted sesame oil, for drizzling

4–6 small pak choi/bok choy, halved

1 small handful of coriander/cilantro leaves

2 tsp toasted sesame or black sesame seeds

This dish is low in fat, amazingly filling and is something different to make with those chicken fillets that always find their way into your shopping basket. You poach the chicken in an Asian-style stock – which keeps the fillets lovely and tender and packs them full of flavour. I always serve the chicken with soba noodles, as they are quick to cook, high in fibre and gluten free (which is a must for some and a bonus for many as wheat can make them a little bloated).

Lightly bash the thick ends of the lemongrass stalks with the base of a saucepan or rolling pin – this will help release their flavour. Put in a high-sided, non-stick frying pan with the stock, fish sauce, lime juice, chilli, lime leaves, ginger and sugar. Gently bring to the boil over a medium heat, then simmer gently for 5 minutes, letting the flavours infuse.

Add the chicken breasts and cover with a lid. Cook for 4 minutes, then turn the chicken over and cook for a further 4 minutes until cooked through.

Meanwhile, cook the noodles in a separate pan of boiling water according to the packet instructions. Drain well and toss in a little sesame oil. Cover and keep warm.

Remove the chicken from the pan with a slotted spoon and leave to rest, covered with foil. Add the pak choi/bok choy to the poaching liquid and simmer for 2–3 minutes until the stems are tender.

Divide the pak choi/bok choy and chicken among plates or bowls. Spoon over the poaching liquid and add the coriander/cilantro. Scatter with the sesame seeds and serve with the noodles.

＊ WHY NOT TRY...

Soba noodles are a good base for salads. Cook according to the packet instructions and cool under cold running water. Drain well and toss with finely sliced peppers, carrot, mange tout/snow peas and spring onions/scallions. Add roughly chopped peanuts or cashew nuts, coriander/cilantro or mint leaves and a dressing made with 1 part rice vinegar, ¼ part caster/granulated sugar and a splash of fish sauce.

spanish chicken, almond and fennel stew

SERVES 4

preparation time: 15 minutes

cooking time: 1¼ hours

200g/7oz/1½ cups whole
blanched almonds

2 tbsp olive oil

8 large skinless, boneless
chicken thighs, each
cut into 3 pieces

1 large fennel bulb,
thinly sliced

1 red onion, sliced

1 red pepper, deseeded
and thinly sliced

1 bay leaf

4 garlic cloves, crushed

1 tsp smoked paprika

a pinch of saffron
strands, soaked in
1 tbsp water

400g/14oz canned
chopped tomatoes

400ml/14fl oz/1²⁄₃ cups
chicken stock

75g/2½oz/heaped ½ cup
pitted green olives

600g/1lb 5oz canned
butter/lima beans,
drained

1 large handful of flat leaf
parsley, leaves roughly
chopped

sea salt and freshly
ground black pepper

We all love 'one-pot' recipes as it means less washing up – this one is good for you, too, and tastes incredible. The generous quantity of almonds give the stew a lovely crunch. If you can, it's well worth using Spanish marcona almonds as they have a slightly sweeter flavour and creamier texture than standard almonds. However, whichever you use, you will still gain from their health benefits. Almonds are a high-protein nut (though technically not a nut but a seed from the fruit of the almond tree) that are rich in mono-saturated fats (a good fat linked with a reduced risk of heart disease) and one of the richest sources of vitamin E, which is pretty useful for protecting against UV light damage.

Heat a flameproof casserole over a medium heat and add the almonds. Stir for about 2 minutes until they start to become lightly golden. Remove from the casserole and leave to one side.

Increase the heat to high and add the olive oil to the casserole. When hot, add the chicken pieces and fry for about 2–3 minutes until golden. Remove with a slotted spoon and add to the almonds.

Reduce the heat to medium. Add the fennel, onion and red pepper and fry for 10 minutes until the vegetables are softened. Stir in the bay leaf, garlic and paprika and return the chicken and almonds to the pan. Fry for about 1 minute, then add the saffron and its soaking liquid, chopped tomatoes, stock and olives. Bring to a simmer, then cover with a lid, reduce the heat to medium-low and cook for 40 minutes, stirring a couple of times during cooking.

Add the butter/lima beans and simmer, uncovered, for a further 15 minutes until thickened and the chicken is cooked through. Remove the bay leaf, stir in the chopped parsley, season with salt and pepper and serve.

spring chicken casserole

SERVES 4

preparation time: 15 minutes
cooking time: 50 minutes

1 tbsp olive oil

4 skinless, boneless
  chicken breast fillets

12–16 shallots, peeled
  and halved

1 large or 2 small fennel
  bulbs, cut into wedges,
  or 150g/5½oz baby
  fennel, halved

250g/9oz new potatoes,
  halved if large

200g/7oz baby carrots,
  halved lengthways

1 bay leaf

2–3 thyme sprigs

peeled zest of ½ lemon

1 heaped tbsp tomato
  purée/paste

500ml/17fl oz/2 cups hot
  chicken stock

200g/7oz asparagus tips

150–200g/5½–7oz/3–4
  cups baby spinach leaves

sea salt and freshly
  ground black pepper

Put a spring in your step with this light, delicate casserole. The colours are fantastic and the chicken is really juicy. To make it perfect, I recommend using fresh chicken stock and buying a good-quality chicken from the butcher – it really does make a huge difference. The thing I love most about this dish is that it's great for a midweek meal and is easily posh enough to serve as a dinner party dish.

Preheat the oven to 190°C/375°F/gas 5. Heat the olive oil in a large flameproof casserole over a high heat. Season the chicken with salt and pepper, add to the casserole and fry for about 2–3 minutes until browned all over. Transfer the chicken to a plate.

Add the shallots to the casserole and fry for just a couple of minutes until they are beginning to turn golden. Stir in the fennel, potatoes, carrots, bay leaf, thyme, lemon zest, tomato purée/paste and salt and pepper, then return the chicken to the casserole. Pour in the stock and bring to a simmer over a high heat, then cover with the lid and bake for 30 minutes.

Add the asparagus to the casserole, cover again with the lid and return to the oven for a further 15 minutes, until the vegetables are tender and the chicken is cooked through.

To serve, divide the spinach leaves into bowls. Top with the chicken breasts, add the vegetables (removing the bay leaf and thyme stalks) and spoon over the liquid, wilting the spinach leaves.

* WASTE NOT, WANT NOT

Any leftover casserole can be easily transformed into a hearty
chicken and vegetable soup. Roughly chop the chicken and
put in a blender with the vegetables and any liquid. Blend
until smooth, adding any extra chicken stock to give you
a thick soup consistency. Gently bring to a simmer over a
medium-low heat. Season to taste and serve.

lemon and garlic griddled chicken with green mash

SERVES 4

preparation time: 20 minutes, plus at least 30 minutes marinating

cooking time: 15 minutes

4 skinless, boneless chicken breast fillets
juice and zest of
  1 large lemon
4 garlic cloves, crushed
2 tbsp olive oil
sea salt and freshly ground black pepper

For the mash:
1 tbsp olive oil
1 large leek, finely diced
2 courgettes/zucchini, finely diced
800g/1lb 12oz canned cannellini beans, drained
150g/5½oz/1 cup frozen peas, defrosted
125ml/4fl oz/½ cup hot chicken stock
1 bunch of basil, leaves and stalks finely chopped
50g/1¾oz/½ cup finely grated Parmesan cheese
2 tbsp extra virgin olive oil

This is a pretty good meal to fall back on when you want a simple and easy-to-prepare dinner. Most of the ingredients can be found in your store cupboard (any canned white beans will work, and frozen broad/fava beans can be used instead of peas) and there isn't really any need to make anything else to go with this. I do, however, quite like some grilled/broiled tomatoes if I have any available. If you have the time, try and marinade the chicken before cooking. Marinating in lemon zest, juice and plenty of garlic not only gives a delicious flavour, but also the acidic lemon juice tenderizes the chicken, keeping it really moist when cooked. I prefer to flatten the chicken breasts out beforehand, as this will ensure even and faster cooking. It's a good thing to do if you have any frustrations you need to alleviate!

Put the chicken between two pieces of baking parchment and gently bash with a rolling pin to flatten to an even thickness. Put in a non-metallic dish.

Mix together the lemon zest and juice, garlic and olive oil and season well with salt and pepper. Rub all over the chicken, cover and leave to marinate in the refrigerator for at least 30 minutes, though up to 2 hours would be good.

To make the mash, heat the olive oil in a saucepan over a medium heat and gently cook the leek and courgettes/zucchini for about 8 minutes until softened but not coloured. Stir in the cannellini beans, peas and stock and cook for a further 2–3 minutes until the beans and peas are hot all the way through. Mash well using a potato masher, or better still use a hand-held/immersion blender to form a chunky purée. Stir in the basil, Parmesan and extra virgin olive oil and season to taste. Keep hot while cooking the chicken.

Heat a griddle/grill pan (or barbecue) until smoking hot, then add the chicken and cook for 2–3 minutes on each side (in batches, if necessary), until cooked through and charred.

Serve the chicken with the hot mash.

moroccan baked chicken parcels

4 skinless, boneless
   chicken breast fillets
4 garlic cloves, crushed
1 tbsp grated root ginger
800g/1lb 12oz/3¼
   cups canned chopped
   tomatoes
800g/1lb 12oz canned
   chickpeas, drained
100g/3½oz/¾ cup
   raisins, sultanas/golden
   raisins or chopped
   apricots
200g/7oz green beans
   (optional)
2 tsp harissa paste
1 tsp ground coriander
1 tsp ground cinnamon
1 large handful of pitted
   black or green olives

To serve:
35g/1¼oz/¼ cup shelled
   pistachio nuts, roughly
   chopped
1 small bunch of fresh
   coriander/cilantro,
   roughly chopped

When life's a bit hectic, this is quite often my go to recipe, because it has a really quick prep time (you can also prepare it several hours before you need it). All the ingredients are put into foil or parchment parcels (or even shop-bought baking bags if you have any), then kept in the refrigerator to be cooked later, or popped straight into the oven. This is a complete meal in one – so there's no need to make extra side dishes. You can, however, throw some extra veg into the parcel, such as fine green beans, small florets of broccoli or asparagus tips. The dish is low in fat and high in protein, and will really fill you up.

Preheat the oven to 220°C/425°F/gas 7 and put a large baking sheet in the oven to heat up. Take a piece of baking parchment or foil about 30 x 60cm/12 x 24in long and fold in half to make a square. Tightly fold together to seal two of the edges, creating a pouch, making sure there are no gaps for the food to escape when cooking. Repeat with another three pieces of baking parchment or foil. (Alternatively, you can buy baking bags from supermarkets that are all ready to use and a real time-saver.)

Slice each chicken breast into 3–4 pieces, and leave to one side.

In a large bowl, mix together all of the remaining ingredients. Divide the mixture evenly among the 4 parcels and put 1 sliced chicken breast into each, pushing down into the sauce to cover. Seal the parcels by folding over the open top, or using an ovenproof tie, leaving some air in them for steam to circulate when cooking.

Put the parcels on the hot baking sheet, slightly spaced apart, and cook for 25 minutes until the chicken is tender, juicy and cooked through and the sauce is thickened. Split open the parcels and serve scattered with the pistachios and coriander/cilantro.

⁎ WASTE NOT, WANT NOT

Why not try mixing any leftover harissa with low-fat Greek yogurt, a squeeze of lemon juice and some finely chopped deseeded cucumber for a refreshing dip or dressing? Or make a spicy tomato sauce for griddled/grilled fish by briefly frying a handful of halved cherry tomatoes in 1 tablespoon extra virgin olive oil. Add 1 teaspoon capers, ½ teaspoon harissa, a squeeze of lemon juice and ½ tablespoon chopped coriander/cilantro, mint or parsley (serves 1).

chicken and date tagine with cauliflower couscous

preparation time: 20 minutes
cooking time: 1 hour 10 minutes

800g/1lb 12oz skinless, boneless chicken thigh fillets, halved
2 onions, finely chopped
4 garlic cloves, crushed
1 tbsp grated root ginger
a pinch of saffron strands
½ tsp ground turmeric
1 cinnamon stick
½ tsp cayenne pepper
2 tbsp olive oil
500ml/17fl oz/2 cups chicken stock
juice of 1 lemon
300g/10½oz/heaped 1⅔ cups pitted dates, preferably Medjool, roughly chopped
30g/1oz/⅓ cup flaked/ sliced almonds
sea salt and freshly ground black pepper

For the cauliflower couscous:
1 large cauliflower
2 tbsp olive oil
juice of ½ lemon
1 small bunch coriander/ cilantro, chopped

After tucking into this you should be feeling full of energy. Dates are known to provide instant energy in the form of natural glucose and are also one of the best sources of potassium (containing up to three times more than bananas). They're also full of dietary fibre, iron, vitamin A, magnesium and many B vitamins. Not bad for a wrinkly brown fruit. As for the extremely tasty couscous – well, it's basically just blitzed up cauliflower that's briefly sautéed and flavoured with lemon and coriander and is light, high in nutrients and not nearly as filling as couscous.

Set a large flameproof casserole over a medium heat and add the chicken, onions, garlic, ginger, spices and olive oil. Mix to coat the chicken in all of the onion mixture and cover with a lid. Cook for 15 minutes, stirring frequently, until the chicken is browned and the onions are golden.

Add the stock and lemon juice and bring to a simmer. Reduce the heat to low, cover with a lid and cook for 35 minutes. Stir in the dates, then cook, uncovered, for a further 15 minutes until the chicken is cooked through.

Meanwhile, heat a frying pan over a medium heat and toast the almonds for a few minutes, stirring occasionally, until they are light golden. Remove from the pan and leave to cool.

To make the 'couscous', cut the cauliflower into quarters and remove the core. Put half of the cauliflower in a food processor and pulse until it resembles couscous. Be careful not to over-blitz at this stage. Transfer to a bowl and repeat with the remaining cauliflower.

Heat a large frying pan over a high heat and add the olive oil. Add the cauliflower couscous and toss and move around in the pan for 3–4 minutes to very lightly cook the cauliflower. Add the lemon juice and coriander/ cilantro, season with salt and pepper and toss to combine.

Season the tagine, scatter with the toasted almonds and serve with the cauliflower couscous.

✳ WASTE NOT, WANT NOT
The cauliflower stalk is full of flavour and can be used to make soup or even cut into small pieces and added to a stir-fry or mashed potato for additional flavour.

preparation time: 15 minutes

cooking time: 1 hour

coriander and coconut chicken curry

4 garlic cloves

2 green bird's eye chillies

5cm/2in piece of root ginger, peeled

1 very large bunch (about 100g/3½oz/2½ cups) of coriander/cilantro, leaves and stalks

400ml/14fl oz/1⅔ cups low fat coconut milk

2 tbsp coconut oil

800g/1lb 12oz skinless, boneless chicken thighs, diced

1 large onion, finely sliced

6 cardamom pods, lightly crushed

1 cinnamon stick

1 tbsp garam masala

10 curry leaves, fresh or dried

2 tsp tamarind paste

150g/5½oz/3 cups baby spinach leaves

basmati rice or wholemeal/whole-wheat chapattis, to serve

sea salt

This is a vibrant green curry that will knock your socks off. Not in heat, but from the wonderful combination of coriander/cilantro, aromatic spices, creamy coconut milk and the fresh spinach stirred through at the end. Just by the colour alone you know this is going to be good for you. I like to serve the curry with basmati rice or some wholemeal/whole-wheat chapattis to soak up the lovely fragrant sauce.

Put the garlic, chillies and ginger in a food processor or blender and whizz to make a chunky paste. Transfer to a bowl and leave to one side.

Put the coriander/cilantro and coconut milk in the processor or blender (it's not necessary to clean it out first). Whizz together to form a vibrant green liquid.

Heat a large pan over a high heat and add the coconut oil. When hot, add the chicken pieces and fry until browned all over. Remove from the pan with a slotted spoon to a plate. Add the onion to the pan and cook for about 5 minutes until softened. Add the garlic, chilli and ginger paste, cardamom pods and cinnamon stick. Fry for 1 minute before stirring in the chicken (including any resting juices), garam masala, curry leaves and coriander/cilantro coconut milk.

Bring to a simmer, then reduce the heat to low, cover with a lid and cook for 45 minutes, stirring a couple of times during cooking, until the chicken is cooked through.

Stir in the tamarind paste, then stir in the spinach leaves a few handfuls at a time until they are wilted. Season with salt and serve with basmati rice or chapattis.

spicy pork goulash with braised wild rice

2 tsp caraway seeds

2 tbsp plain/all-purpose flour

2 tsp smoked paprika

600g/1lb 5oz pork fillet, cut into chunks

2 tbsp olive oil

1 large onion, finely sliced

4 garlic cloves, crushed

1 red and 1 green pepper, deseeded and finely chopped

1 long red chilli, deseeded and finely chopped

1 tsp dried oregano

400g/14oz/1⅔ cups canned plum tomatoes

1 tbsp red wine vinegar

200ml/7fl oz/scant 1 cup beef stock

4 tbsp low-fat yogurt

sea salt and freshly ground black pepper

For the wild rice:

1 tbsp olive oil

1 onion, chopped

2 garlic cloves, crushed

1 bay leaf

250g/9oz/1¼ cups mixed wild and basmati rice

500ml/17fl oz/2 cups vegetable or chicken stock

150g/5½oz/3 cups baby spinach leaves

This lighter version of the classic comfort dish won't disappoint. It contains less saturated fat by using yogurt rather than sour cream, and I use a lean cut of pork. Plus you'll get plenty of flavour from the generous amount of herbs and spices in the sauce. You can serve it with plain rice, but the braised wild rice adds a lovely flavour and texture, not to mention more health benefits. Wild rice is in fact a grain (the seed of wheatgrass) and contains more protein, zinc and potassium than white or brown rice and is also rich in antioxidants and essential vitamins.

Preheat the oven to 180°C/350°C/gas 4. Lightly toast the caraway seeds in a dry frying pan over a medium heat for about 30–60 seconds until they become aromatic. Remove from the heat and lightly crush in a pestle and mortar. Leave to one side.

Combine the flour and 1 teaspoon of the paprika on a plate and season with salt and pepper. Toss the pork in the flour. Heat a large flameproof casserole over a high heat and add the oil. When the oil is shimmering hot, add the pork and fry for about 3–4 minutes until it is browned all over. Remove from the casserole using a slotted spoon and leave to one side.

Reduce the heat to medium-low and stir the onion and garlic into the casserole. Fry for about 8 minutes until softened, adding a splash of water to the pan to help prevent the onion from sticking. Add the red and green peppers, chilli, half of the crushed caraway seeds and the oregano. Continue to cook for a minute or so before adding the tomatoes, red wine vinegar and beef stock. Return the pork to the casserole and bring to a simmer. Cover with a lid and transfer to the oven for 1½ hours, stirring a couple of times during cooking.

To braise the rice, set a separate flameproof casserole or dish with a lid over a medium heat. Add the olive oil and when hot, gently sauté the onion for about 10 minutes until softened but not coloured. Add the garlic, bay leaf and rice and cook for a further minute, then add the stock and salt and pepper. Bring to the boil over a high heat and cover with the lid. Transfer to the oven for 20 minutes until the rice is tender and the stock has been absorbed. When cooked, stir in the spinach leaves until wilted.

Stir together the yogurt and the remaining paprika. Spoon over the cooked goulash, sprinkle with the reserved caraway seeds and serve with the braised wild rice.

preparation time: 10 minutes

cooking time: 10 minutes

stir-fried chilli beef and rice noodles

200g/7oz flat rice
  noodles
2 tbsp rapeseed/canola
  oil
600g/1lb 5oz sirloin
  steak, fat trimmed and
  thinly sliced
1½ red chillies, finely
  sliced
5cm/2in piece of root
  ginger, peeled and
  chopped
2 garlic cloves, crushed
200g/7oz shredded kale,
  spring/collard greens,
  green savoy cabbage or
  chard
150g/5½oz mange tout/
  snow peas or sugar snap
  peas
4 spring onions/
  scallions, cut into
  pieces diagonally
1 tbsp toasted sesame
  seeds
1 handful of coriander/
  cilantro leaves, roughly
  chopped

For the sauce:
2 tbsp soy sauce
3 tbsp oyster sauce
1 tbsp rice vinegar
2 tsp honey
1 tsp cornflour/
  cornstarch

If you are after a quick meal then a stir-fry is always a good choice. You can use other vegetables or meat depending on what you have available or like. The rich flavoured sauce does work particularly well with beef and the robust leafy greens. The best thing you can do when cooking a stir-fry is to get everything prepared before you start cooking, and then before you know it, this iron-rich, energy-giving stir-fry will be ready to eat. Make sure you have serving plates and cutlery ready, too – then as soon as it's cooked you can eat.

Mix together all of the sauce ingredients with 4 tablespoons water and leave to one side.

Cook the rice noodles according to the packet instructions. Drain and refresh under cold running water. Leave to one side.

Heat a wok over a high heat until it is very hot. Add half of the oil and swirl around to coat the surface of the wok. Add the steak and half of the chilli. Toss in the pan for about 1 minute until the steak has browned, then remove from the wok. Add the remaining chilli, ginger and garlic. Stir-fry for about 1 minute, then add your chosen greens and the peas. Toss around in the pan for 1½–2 minutes, adding a splash of water to create some steam to cook the veg. Add the spring onions/scallions and return the beef and any resting juices to the wok. Stir-fry for 1 minute or so to completely heat through. Divide evenly onto plates or into bowls and scatter with sesame seeds and coriander/cilantro.

Quickly return the wok to the heat and add the remaining oil. Toss in the cooked rice noodles, then pour in the sauce. Stir-fry for 1 minute or so until the sauce thickens and coats the noodles. Divide among the plates or bowls, spooning over any sauce left in the wok, and serve immediately.

SERVES 4

preparation time: 20 minutes
cooking time: 15 minutes

kale pesto pasta with crispy prosciutto

300–400g/10½–14oz
  pasta
200g/7oz cherry
  tomatoes on the vine
olive oil, for drizzling
12 prosciutto slices
sea salt and freshly
  ground black pepper
extra virgin olive oil,
  to serve

For the kale pesto:
50g/1¾oz/⅓ cup pine
  nuts
100g/3½oz prepared kale
  leaves (stripped from
  the stalks)
1 large garlic clove,
  roughly chopped
1 large bunch of basil,
  leaves only
50g/1¾oz/½ cup grated
  Parmesan cheese
100ml/3½fl oz/scant
  ½ cup olive oil

Pesto pasta is a really quick and easy midweek meal that many households will no doubt turn to on a regular basis. But to make the pesto a little more nutritious, I use kale, a genuine superfood, in place of some of the basil. Its flavour and colour are amazing, and it can be used in all the same ways as traditional pesto. You could also try replacing the kale with watercress, rocket/arugula or baby spinach leaves, if you've a bag in the refrigerator that you need to use up. They won't need blanching first and have an equally delicious flavour. Try using whole-wheat pasta, if you haven't already.

Heat a small frying pan over a medium heat and add the pine nuts. Toss around in the pan for a couple of minutes until lightly golden. Remove from the pan and leave to cool.

Bring a large saucepan of water to the boil over a high heat and add a good pinch of salt. Fill a bowl with ice-cold water and leave to one side. Put the kale into the boiling water and cook for 1 minute. Remove with a slotted spoon and transfer to the iced water to instantly cool down.

Return the water in the pan to the boil, add the pasta and cook for 10–12 minutes, or until al dente.

Meanwhile, drain the kale and squeeze out the water. Put in a food processor with the remaining pesto ingredients. Blitz to a pesto consistency, adding a splash of the pasta cooking water to loosen if it seems too thick. Season to taste with salt and pepper.

Preheat the grill/broiler to high. Put the tomatoes on a baking sheet, drizzle with a little olive oil and season with salt and pepper. Lay the prosciutto next to the tomatoes and place under the hot grill/broiler for 3–4 minutes, turning the prosciutto halfway through. Remove from the grill/broiler when the prosciutto is crisp and the tomatoes are starting to burst.

Drain the pasta and toss in as much pesto as you like. Spoon onto plates and top with the tomatoes and crispy prosciutto. Add a drizzle of extra virgin olive oil and a twist of pepper and serve.

✳ *PS...* If you have not used up all the pesto, it will keep in the refrigerator for up to 1 week (add a thin layer of olive oil on top to preserve). Alternatively, it also freezes very well for up to 1 month.

preparation time: 20 minutes,
plus 30 minutes chilling
cooking time: 30 minutes

beef and quinoa meatballs

250g/9oz lean minced/
  ground beef
250g/9oz cooked and
  cooled quinoa (see page
  124)
3 tbsp chia seeds
2 garlic cloves, crushed
1 tbsp black olive
  tapenade
1 egg, lightly beaten
1 tsp paprika
1 long red chilli, finely
  chopped
1 tbsp olive oil
pasta or couscous, to
  serve

*For the aubergine and
  tomato sauce:*
2 tbsp olive oil
1 onion, finely chopped
1 aubergine/eggplant,
  finely diced
250ml/9fl oz/1 cup red
  wine
400g/14oz/scant 1²⁄₃
  cups canned chopped
  tomatoes
2 tbsp tomato purée/
  paste
1 tsp caster/granulated
  sugar
1 tbsp red wine vinegar
1 large handful of
  chopped basil, plus
  extra leaves to serve
sea salt and freshly
  ground black pepper

Forget the spag bol for once and opt for something a bit different. These meatballs are full of flavour and goodness due to the addition of quinoa, which makes them light in comparison to all beef (and lower in saturated fat) and not too filling. I've also added chia seeds into the mix, which act as a binding agent to the meatballs, giving them an even healthier boost. Serve with pasta (whole-wheat is great), couscous or some oven-baked potato wedges.

To make the meatballs, put all the ingredients except the olive oil in a large bowl. Season with salt and pepper and mix well. Using wet hands, divide the mixture into about 20 balls, shaping and squeezing lightly. Chill for 30 minutes.

To make the sauce, heat the olive oil in a flameproof casserole or large saucepan over a medium heat. Fry the onion for 5 minutes until starting to soften. Add the aubergine/eggplant and continue to fry for further a 5 minutes. Increase the heat to high, pour in the red wine and allow to bubble away for about 30 seconds, then stir in the tomatoes, tomato purée/paste, vinegar and 125ml/4fl oz/½ cup water. Season with salt and pepper. Bring to the boil, then reduce the heat to low, cover with a lid and simmer for 10 minutes.

Meanwhile, heat the olive oil in a large frying pan over a medium-high heat and when hot, fry the meatballs for 8–10 minutes until golden, turning during cooking so that they are browned all over.

Gently stir the meatballs and chopped basil into the tomato sauce. Cook for 10 minutes, loosely covered with a lid, until the meatballs are cooked through. Serve the meatballs with pasta or couscous, scattered with extra basil leaves.

PS... Once you've given these a try, you can play around with different flavour combinations. Try Greek-inspired meatballs, using lean minced/ground lamb, ground cinnamon and cumin and chopped oregano, and serve with bulgur wheat. Or make Moroccan meatballs flavoured with ground coriander, harissa paste, grated root ginger and chopped dried apricots, and serve with couscous.

queen quinoa

It's hard to imagine a time when quinoa (pronounced 'keen-wah') wasn't widely available, yet now you can get hold of it pretty much anywhere and everywhere. It's become increasingly popular over the years and is one of the healthiest and most versatile ingredients I can think of.

nutritional benefits

Quinoa is often referred to as an 'ancient grain' or 'mother grain'. It is native to South America and has been cultivated for more than 5,000 years. Even though it is called a grain and is often used in the same way as other wholegrains, in fact it is a highly nutritious gluten-free seed from a vegetable related to spinach. It is a complete protein and also high in magnesium, iron, fibre and many vitamins, and it contains virtually no fat. The fact that it is incredibly easy and quick to cook and tastes delicious makes quinoa a healthy store-cupboard must-have, all year round.

types of quinoa

There are many types of quinoa, but the main three are white/yellow (most widely available), red and black. All can be cooked in exactly the same way, although red holds its shape slightly better and black is a bit earthier and sweeter in flavour. You can also get quinoa flakes (see my recipe for porridge/oatmeal using them on page 26) and quinoa flour, which can be bought in its dry form and used in products such as quinoa pasta.

how to cook

Quinoa as a 'grain' is best cooked using an absorption method very similar to rice. Use a ratio of 2:1 water to quinoa. Dry quinoa will cook to three or four times its original volume, so for example, 2 cups water and 1 cup quinoa will give you up to 4 cups of cooked quinoa, or approximately 4 servings.

Rinsing: Before cooking, it is a good idea to rinse quinoa in a sieve/strainer under fast-running cold water. This will wash away a natural coating on the outside of the 'grain' that can give a bitter taste. It's not essential and some people don't pick up on the bitter taste, so if you don't have the time or think this stage is a pain, then it's just fine to use straight out of the packet.

Toasting: This is purely an optional stage when cooking quinoa, but it will enhance the natural nuttiness. Toast for 1 minute or so in a saucepan either with or without a drop or two of oil.

Cooking: Add the measured water and a pinch of salt to the toasted or untoasted quinoa over a high heat. Bring to the boil. Boil rapidly for 2 minutes, then reduce the heat to low. Cover with a lid and leave to cook for 12 minutes. Remove from the heat and, leaving the lid on, leave to stand for 5 minutes. Remove the lid and gently fluff with a fork. The 'grain' will be translucent and the white spirals will separate from the 'grain'.

ADDITIONAL FLAVOURS:
- » Use stock as an alternative to water – chicken, vegetable, lamb or fish, depending on what you are serving your quinoa with.
- » Spices – such as saffron strands, cinnamon, cloves, cardamom, star anise, curry leaves.
- » Herbs – fresh sprigs of rosemary, thyme, oregano, parsley, bay.

what to make

- » Use quinoa 'grains' in recipes as you would rice, pasta, couscous, bulgur wheat or other grains.
- » Flaked quinoa can be used an alternative to oats in porridge/oatmeal.
- » I've used quinoa in numerous recipes in this book, such as my Rich Vegetarian Chilli with Spiced Walnut Butter (see page 163) or Beef and Quinoa Meatballs served with aubergine and tomato sauce (see page 122).

beef, squash and mango pilau

1 handful of flaked
   coconut
1 tbsp olive oil
400g/14oz beef stewing
   steak, diced
1 large onion, finely
   sliced
5cm/2in piece of root
   ginger, peeled and
   grated
4 garlic cloves, crushed
1 green chilli, chopped
3 tbsp medium curry
   powder
300g/10½oz/heaped 1½
   cups brown basmati rice
750ml/26fl oz/3 cups hot
   beef stock
400ml/14fl oz/1⅔ cups
   low-fat coconut milk
½ butternut squash,
   about 650g/1lb 6oz,
   peeled and cut into
   3cm/1¼in cubes
1 small bunch of
   coriander/cilantro,
   chopped
1 large ripe mango,
   peeled, pitted and diced
sea salt and freshly
   ground black pepper

This is another one of my go to dishes for a cold day. It ticks all the boxes for comfort food – spicy, hearty, rich and satisfying, yet it's still really healthy. It's a full-flavoured one-pot wonder with a refreshing bite (due to the juicy mango) and a crunchy coconut finish.

Preheat the oven to 180°C/350°F/gas 4. Heat a frying pan over a medium heat and toast the coconut for a few minutes, stirring occasionally, until light golden. Remove from the pan and leave to cool.

Heat the oil in a large, shallow ovenproof pan with a lid over a high heat. When hot, add the beef and cook for about 1 minute, turning frequently, until brown all over. Remove with a slotted spoon to a plate, then add the onion, ginger, garlic and chilli to the pan. Fry for about 5 minutes, adding a splash of water if the pan seems a little dry.

Stir in the curry powder and rice. Fry for a couple of minutes, then return the beef to the pan. Pour in the stock and coconut milk and bring to the boil. Cover with a lid, then transfer to the oven for 20 minutes.

Remove from the oven. Stir in the butternut squash and season with salt and pepper. Cover again with the lid, return to the oven and cook for 20 minutes until the liquid has been absorbed and the rice and squash are tender. Leave to stand, covered, for 10 minutes.

Sprinkle over the chopped coriander/cilantro and gently mix in using a fork. Serve the pilau scattered with the mango and toasted coconut.

*WASTE NOT, WANT NOT

If you're not sure what to do with a leftover half of butternut squash, now you have an excuse to make some chocolate brownies. Check out the recipe for Chocolate Pumpkin Brownies on page 214. Use the squash instead of pumpkin to make a purée that gets swirled through a chocolatey batter.

middle eastern lamb with kale and prunes

2 tbsp olive or rapeseed/
  canola oil

450g/1lb diced lean lamb
  shoulder

1 large onion, finely
  chopped

1 large carrot, finely
  chopped

4 garlic cloves, finely
  chopped

2 red chillies, finely
  chopped

1 tbsp ground cumin

400g/14oz canned
  chickpeas, drained

400g/14oz/scant 1⅔
  cups canned chopped
  tomatoes

500ml/17fl oz/2 cups
  lamb stock

200g/7oz/1 cup prunes,
  halved

225g/8oz kale, tough
  stalks removed and
  leaves roughly chopped

40g/1½oz/¼ cup pine
  nuts

juice and finely grated
  zest of ½ lemon

1 small bunch of mint
  leaves, roughly chopped

sea salt and freshly
  ground black pepper

bulgur wheat or
  couscous, to serve

I don't know where to begin when describing this dish! It is such a tasty stew, overflowing with beautiful flavours and goodness. I often make this ahead of time and then gently heat through when I need it, adding the kale for the last 10 minutes of cooking to keep it as fresh and flavoursome as possible. I then serve it with the lemon zest, mint and toasted pine nuts scattered over the top for a final burst of flavour and colour. It's lovely served with bulgur wheat or couscous – I've also served it with mashed root veg, which went down pretty well, too.

Heat 1 tablespoon of the olive oil in a flameproof casserole over a high heat. Season the lamb and fry for about 2–3 minutes until golden brown all over. Remove with a slotted spoon and leave to one side. Add the remaining oil to the pan with the onion and carrot. Reduce the heat to medium and cook until the onion is lightly golden.

Stir in the garlic, chillies and cumin and return the lamb to the pan. Cook for about 1 minute, then stir in the chickpeas, chopped tomatoes and stock. Bring to the boil, then reduce the heat to low, cover with a lid and cook for 30 minutes.

Stir in the prunes, cover again with the lid and cook for a further 30 minutes. Add the kale and cook, uncovered, for 10 minutes.

Meanwhile, heat a small frying pan over a medium heat and add the pine nuts. Toss around in the pan for a couple of minutes until lightly golden, then remove from the pan and leave to cool.

Stir the lemon juice into the stew and season with salt and pepper. Scatter with the lemon zest, mint and toasted pine nuts and serve with bulgur wheat or couscous.

lamb and chickpea koftas with sesame carrot mash

SERVES 4

preparation time: 25 minutes

cooking time: 25 minutes

400g/14oz canned
   chickpeas, drained
1 onion, roughly
   chopped
4 garlic cloves, roughly
   chopped
1 tsp ground cinnamon
1 tsp ground cumin
1 red chilli, roughly
   chopped
zest of 1 lemon
250g/9oz lean minced/
   ground lamb
olive oil, for frying
sea salt and freshly
   ground black pepper

For the sesame carrot mash:
1 kg/2lb 4oz carrots,
   peeled and sliced
3 tbsp tahini, plus extra
   for drizzling
1 tbsp lemon juice
2 tbsp extra virgin olive
   oil
1 small bunch of flat leaf
   parsley, chopped

To serve:
2 tsp sesame seeds
1 tsp cumin seeds
lemon wedges

Although traditionally koftas are served with flatbreads or couscous, I've opted to serve mine with a nutrient-rich carrot mash flavoured with tangy lemon juice, parsley and lots of tahini (sesame seed paste). Sesame seeds are rich in many essential minerals including calcium, zinc and iron. Although you can easily buy tahini in supermarkets, I do thoroughly recommend having a go at making your own (see page 21) – it's very simple and the flavour is amazing.

To make the koftas, put all of the ingredients except the lamb and olive oil in a food processor and pulse until chopped together, but not a paste. Tip into a large bowl, add the lamb and season well with salt and pepper. Using your hands, bring everything together, then divide into 8 rough sausage shapes. Firmly squeeze and shape each sausage around a presoaked wooden skewer and chill until needed.

For the mash, steam the carrots over a pan of boiling water for about 15 minutes, or until tender. Transfer to a bowl and mash together with the tahini, lemon juice and extra virgin olive oil. Season with salt and pepper. Stir in the chopped parsley and keep hot.

To cook the koftas, heat a large frying pan or griddle/grill pan over a medium-high heat. Drizzle some olive oil over the koftas and rub in to evenly coat. When the pan is hot, cook the koftas for 8–10 minutes, turning occasionally, until golden and cooked through.

Meanwhile, lightly toast the sesame and cumin seeds in a small frying pan over a medium heat for about 2 minutes, until the sesame seeds are golden and the cumin seeds are aromatic.

Serve the koftas with the sesame carrot mash, scattered with the toasted seeds, drizzled with a little extra tahini and with lemon wedges on the side to squeeze over.

preparation time: 10 minutes
cooking time: 40 minutes

braised venison sausages, puy lentils and chard

8 venison sausages

1½ tbsp olive oil

1 large onion, finely
sliced

2 garlic cloves, finely
sliced

1 red chilli, finely sliced

250g/9oz/1¼ cups Puy
lentils

600ml/21fl oz/2½ cups
hot chicken stock

2 apples, cored and cut
into small chunks

150g/5½oz Swiss chard,
roughly chopped

sea salt and freshly
ground black pepper

Venison sausages have found their way into most butchers and supermarkets, which is great because they make a leaner and healthier alternative to many pork sausages. Earthy and comforting, this wholesome stew can be thrown together pretty quickly and will keep you full for hours. Puy lentils, with their meaty texture, have a very low glycaemic index, which means they release energy at a slow and steady rate. I've used rainbow chard here, which looks great; do, however, try greens such as kale, cabbage, cavolo nero or spinach.

Remove the sausages from the skins and break each sausage into 3–4 chunky pieces. Heat half of the olive oil in a large, shallow ovenproof pan over a high heat and when hot, fry the sausage meat until golden. Remove with a slotted spoon and add the remaining oil. Reduce the heat to medium and stir in the onion, garlic and chilli. Fry for about 8 minutes until the onion is softened and starting to colour.

Return the sausages to the pan with the lentils and stir in, then add the stock and apples. Bring to a simmer, then cover with a lid, reduce the heat to low and cook for 20 minutes until the sausages are cooked through and the lentils are almost tender.

Stir in the chard, a handful at a time, then cook for 5 minutes until the chard is tender. Season with salt and pepper and serve.

*WASTE NOT, WANT NOT

Gently fry any leftover chard in olive oil with chopped garlic and chilli, then add a splash of balsamic. Top with a poached egg and serve with a toasted wholemeal/whole-wheat muffin.

preparation time: 15 minutes, plus 30–60 minutes marinating

cooking time: 8 minutes

steamed soy and lemon fish with vegetable broth

4 thick white fish fillets, such as cod, haddock, pollock or coley, about 150g/5½oz each, skin on

1 tbsp light soy sauce

juice and finely grated zest of 1 small lemon

2.5cm/1in piece of root ginger, peeled and grated

1 tbsp honey

2 garlic cloves, crushed

For the vegetable broth:

875ml/30fl oz/3¾ cups good-quality vegetable stock

150ml/5fl oz/scant ⅔ cup rice wine or dry sherry

100g/3½oz asparagus tips

150g/5½oz baby courgettes/zucchini, halved lengthways

200g/7oz baby carrots, halved lengthways

100g/3½oz baby corn, halved lengthways

100g/3½oz mange tout/ snow peas or sugar snap peas

1 bunch of spring onions/scallions, cut into 1cm/½in lengths

175g/6oz/heaped 1 cup fresh or frozen peas

1 small handful of mint leaves, finely chopped

If you're concerned this may be a little on the light side as there are no added carbohydrates, you can add a portion of cooked noodles or rice to the base of the bowls before spooning over the broth. It's a doddle to make and a lovely alternative midweek meal or even a dinner party option.

Put the fish in a flat non-reactive dish. Mix together all of the remaining fish ingredients and pour over the fish. Leave to marinate for 30–60 minutes, depending on the time you have available, turning halfway through.

Put the stock and rice wine in a saucepan or base of a steamer over a high heat and bring to the boil. Add the asparagus, courgettes/zucchini, carrots and baby corn to the boiling stock. Put the steamer over the top and add the fish, skin side down. Cover with a tight-fitting lid and cook for 5 minutes.

Add the mange tout/snow peas, spring onions/scallions and peas to the rest of the vegetables. Put the steamer back on top and cook for a further 1–2 minutes until all of the vegetables are just tender and the fish is opaque and flakes slightly when lightly pressed.

Scatter the mint over the vegetables and divide evenly into bowls. Top with the fish and serve steaming hot.

laksa seafood parcels

SERVES 4

preparation time: 20 minutes

cooking time: 25 minutes

200g/7oz flat rice
  noodles

250g/9oz skinless white
  fish fillets, such as cod,
  haddock, pollock
  or coley, cut into
  bite-size pieces

200g/7oz raw, peeled
  king prawns/jumbo
  shrimp

200g/7oz scallops

1/3 cucumber, peeled
  and cut into 5mm/1/4in
  thick sticks

150g/5 1/2oz mange tout/
  snow peas

200g/7oz/2 1/2 cups bean
  sprouts

4 tbsp Simple Laksa Paste
  (see below)

4 tsp lime juice

4 tsp fish sauce

400ml/14fl oz/1 2/3 cups
  low-fat coconut milk

100ml/3 1/2fl oz/scant
  1/2 cup fish stock

To serve:

4 spring onions/
  scallions, finely sliced
  diagonally

1 red chilli, deseeded
  and finely sliced

1 small handful of
  coriander/cilantro
  leaves

lime wedges

Though the ingredients list looks long – this is in fact another great dish to prepare when you want something simple, quick and healthy. Steaming everything in the parcels retains all the flavours and more nutrients than many methods of cooking – win win.

Cook the rice noodles according to the packet instructions, but if you can, try to leave them slightly al dente. Drain and refresh under cold running water. Leave to one side.

Preheat the oven to 220°C/425°F/gas 7. Take a piece of baking parchment or foil about 30 x 60cm/12 x 24in long and fold in half to make a square. Tightly fold together to seal two of the edges, creating a pouch, making sure there are no gaps for the food to escape when cooking. Repeat with another three pieces of baking parchment or foil. (Alternatively, you can buy baking bags from supermarkets that are all ready to use and a real time-saver.)

Divide the noodles, fish, prawns/shrimp, scallops, cucumber, mange tout/snow peas and two-thirds of the bean sprouts between the 4 parcels. Mix together the laksa paste, lime juice, fish sauce, coconut milk and stock. Divide evenly into the parcels, then seal them by folding over the open top, or using an ovenproof tie, leaving some air in for steam to circulate when cooking.

Using your hands, give each bag a massage to make sure everything is coated in the liquid, then place directly on the oven rack. Put a baking sheet on the shelf below just in case any liquid escapes (it shouldn't if you have made secure parcels). Cook for 20 minutes until the prawns are pink and the fish is cooked through, giving the bags a shake halfway through.

Remove from the oven and split open each parcel into a bowl. Scatter over the remaining bean sprouts and the spring onions/scallions, chilli and coriander/cilantro. Serve with lime wedges, to squeeze over.

❊ HOW TO MAKE: SIMPLE LAKSA PASTE

You can buy some great-quality laksa curry pastes, but making your own is easy and makes the dish taste that little bit more refined. Simply blitz together 2 red chillies (1 deseeded and 1 with the seeds in), 2 garlic cloves, a 2.5cm/1in piece of peeled root ginger, 4 shallots, 1 lemongrass stalk, 1/2 teaspoon each of ground turmeric, coriander, cumin and paprika, 1 tablespoon fish sauce, 50g/1 3/4oz/1/2 cup ground almonds and 2 tablespoons rapeseed/canola oil. Store in a screw-topped jar in the refrigerator for up to 2 weeks.

SERVES 4

preparation time: 20 minutes, plus 1 hour marinating

cooking time: 25 minutes

tikka baked cod with coconut relish

3 tbsp tikka curry paste

4 tbsp plain yogurt

juice and finely grated zest of ½ lime

4 thick cod fillets, about 150g/5½oz each, skin on

olive oil, for greasing

For the coconut relish:

100g/3½oz fresh coconut flesh, broken into pieces

1 tsp cumin seeds

4 tbsp plain yogurt

1 small bunch of coriander/cilantro

1 green chilli, roughly chopped

juice of ½ lime

sea salt and freshly ground black pepper

For the cucumber salad:

½ cucumber

1 ripe mango

1 small red onion, finely sliced

1 tbsp olive oil

juice of ½ lime

The coconut relish really makes this a bit special. You can get fresh coconuts pretty much anywhere and they offer a fun challenge to open; however, bought ready-shelled coconut is pretty common in supermarkets now if you want to save yourself the time. Coconuts are great for your general health and wellbeing. They support the immune system, provide a natural source of quick energy and improve digestion and absorption of many nutrients. Serve the spicy baked cod, coconut relish and refreshing salad as it is or with some warmed wholemeal/whole-wheat chapattis or brown basmati for a more substantial meal.

For the cod, mix together the curry paste, yogurt and lemon zest and juice in a non-reactive bowl. Add the cod and coat well. Leave to marinate in the refrigerator for up to 1 hour.

Meanwhile, make the coconut relish. Put the coconut flesh in a food processor and blitz until finely chopped. Heat a medium-large frying pan over a medium-high heat and toast the coconut with the cumin seeds for 4–5 minutes until lightly golden and aromatic. Leave to cool.

Preheat the oven to 220°C/425°F/gas 7. Line a baking sheet with foil and lightly oil. Remove the cod from the marinade and put, skin side down, on the prepared baking sheet. Bake for 20 minutes, or until the fish is just cooked through and flakes when lightly pressed.

When the coconut and cumin have cooled, return to the food processor with the remaining relish ingredients. Whizz together until fairly smooth. Season to taste.

To make the salad, cut the cucumber in half lengthways and thinly slice each half diagonally. Put in a large bowl. Peel the mango, remove the pit and cut the flesh into strips. Add to the bowl with the sliced red onion. Toss everything with the olive oil and lime juice, then season.

Serve the cooked cod with the cucumber salad and coconut relish.

tray-baked brill and puy lentils with salsa verde

25g/1oz dried porcini
  mushrooms
250g/9oz/1¼ cups Puy
  lentils
3 tbsp olive oil, plus extra
  for drizzling
1 red onion, finely sliced
1 red pepper, deseeded
  and sliced
250g/9oz/1⅔ cups
  baby plum or cherry
  tomatoes, halved
4 brill fillets, about
  150–175g/5½–6oz each
100g/3½oz/2 cups baby
  spinach leaves
sea salt and freshly
  ground black pepper

For the salsa verde:
1 small bunch of parsley,
  leaves stripped
1 small bunch of basil,
  leaves stripped
1 tbsp capers
4 anchovy fillets
1 garlic clove
1 tbsp lemon juice
4 tbsp olive oil

You can use other white fish for this, such as cod, bream, bass, haddock or pollock. My personal favourite is the meaty texture and delicate flavour of brill. There is a lovely combination of flavours and textures in this dish and it is all finished off nicely when you spoon the tangy, salty, herby salsa verde over the top when serving.

Cover the mushrooms with about 250ml/9fl oz/1 cup hot water and leave to soak for 20 minutes. Cook the lentils in a pan of boiling water for 15–20 minutes until they are tender. Drain well.

Meanwhile, make the salsa verde. Very finely chop the parsley and basil leaves, capers, anchovy fillets and garlic. Put everything in a bowl, mix in the lemon juice and olive oil, and season with salt and pepper. Stir in a little water to loosen to a spoonable consistency, if needed. Leave to one side until you are ready to serve.

Preheat the oven to 200°C/400°F/gas 6. Heat the oil in a roasting pan over a medium heat on the hob/stovetop. Add the onion and red pepper and cook for about 5 minutes until softened but not coloured. Remove from the heat and stir in the cooked lentils and halved tomatoes.

Drain the mushrooms, reserving 185ml/6fl oz/¾ cup of the soaking liquid. Roughly chop the mushrooms, then add the mushrooms and soaking liquor to the roasting pan. Stir everything together.

Top the lentils with the brill, skin side down. Drizzle with a little olive oil, then season everything with salt and pepper. Roast for 15 minutes, or until the fish is cooked through and starting to turn golden.

Gently lift the fish from the tray. Stir the spinach into the lentils until it is wilted. Spoon onto plates, top with the fish and serve with the salsa verde to spoon over.

preparation time: 15 minutes,
plus 30 minutes
marinating
cooking time: 35 minutes

thai salmon skewers with edamame quinoa

700g/1lb 9oz skinless
  salmon fillet, cut into
  2–3cm/¾–1¼in pieces
3 tbsp Thai green curry
  paste
4 tsp fish sauce
juice and zest of 1 large
  juicy lime
1 small handful of flaked
  coconut
200g/7oz/heaped 1 cup
  quinoa
200g/7oz slim stalks of
  broccoli
250g/9oz/scant 2 cups
  frozen edamame beans
  (green soybeans),
  defrosted
1 large handful of
  coriander/cilantro,
  roughly chopped
olive oil, for brushing
lime wedges, to serve

Thai curry pastes don't just have to be used to make a curry. They're ideal to use as a very handy ready-prepared marinade for fish and meat. Here I use green curry paste to coat chunks of salmon before grilling/broiling. If you can, buy a nice thick salmon fillet as it will hold well on the skewers. Other chunky fish such as tuna, cod, pollock or monkfish would work really well, too.

Put the fish in a non-reactive bowl with the curry paste, fish sauce and half of the lime juice and mix everything together. Leave to marinate for about 30 minutes.

Heat a frying pan over a medium heat and toast the coconut flakes for a few minutes, stirring occasionally, until they are light golden. Remove from the pan and leave to cool.

Put the quinoa in a saucepan with 500ml/17fl oz/2 cups water. Set over a high heat and bring to the boil, then cook at a rolling boil for 1 minute. Cover with a lid, reduce the heat to low and leave to cook for 12 minutes. Remove from the heat, leaving the lid on, and leave to stand for a further 5 minutes. Run a fork through to separate the grains.

Steam the broccoli for 4 minutes. Add the edamame and cook with the broccoli for a further 2 minutes until heated through. Remove from the heat and tip into a large bowl. Add the quinoa, chopped coriander/cilantro, lime zest and remaining lime juice. Mix well.

Preheat the grill/broiler to hot. Thread the salmon pieces onto metal skewers (or wooden ones that have been soaked in water so they don't burn). Put on a non-stick baking sheet and brush lightly with oil. Cook under the grill/broiler for 10 minutes, turning occasionally, until golden and cooked through.

Divide the quinoa evenly onto plates, scatter over the toasted coconut flakes and top with the salmon skewers. Serve with lime wedges to squeeze over.

grilled salmon with herby courgette couscous

175g/6oz/1 cup whole-wheat couscous

75g/2½oz/⅔ cup dried cranberries

juice and finely grated zest of 1 lemon

275ml/9½fl oz/scant 1¼ cups hot vegetable stock

4 skinless salmon fillets, about 150g/5½oz each

1 tbsp harissa paste (optional)

300g/10½oz courgettes/zucchini, grated

1 small bunch of dill, chopped

1 small bunch of mint, chopped

80g/2¾oz/heaped ½ cup shelled pistachio nuts, roughly chopped

3 tbsp extra virgin olive oil

2 tsp honey

sea salt and freshly ground black pepper

This is such a refreshing salad that has the added benefit of being fairly quick to prepare. The courgettes/zucchini are kept raw and simply grated, which reveals their soft texture and sweet and slightly nutty flavour. Simple grilled/broiled salmon (or other fish) goes well with the salad but I like to add a kick of spice by spreading over a little harissa paste just before cooking, which complements the sweetness of the cranberries in the salad. Any leftover couscous is great served the next day with some feta cheese crumbled over the top.

Preheat the grill/broiler to high and line a baking sheet with foil.

Put the couscous, cranberries and lemon zest in a large bowl and stir in the hot stock. Stir and cover with a plate or cling film/plastic wrap. Leave to stand for 5–6 minutes until the couscous has absorbed the stock.

Put the salmon on the prepared baking sheet. Season with salt and pepper and spread some harissa paste over the top, if using. Cook under the hot grill/broiler for about 8 minutes until just cooked through and lightly golden on the surface.

Run a fork through the couscous to separate the grains, then stir in the grated courgettes/zucchini, herbs and pistachios.

In a separate bowl, mix together the olive oil, lemon juice and honey. Season with salt and plenty of pepper. Pour over the couscous salad and mix well, then serve with the salmon.

preparation time: 10 minutes
cooking time: 10 minutes

seeded baked salmon with crushed minty peas

4 tbsp mixed seeds, such
  as sesame, flaxseed, chia
  and crushed hemp
1 tbsp wasabi paste
4 thick salmon fillets,
  about 150g/5½oz each,
  skin on
olive oil, for frying
lemon wedges, to serve

For the minty peas:
125ml/4fl oz/½ cup
  chicken stock
1 garlic clove, crushed
450g/1lb/3 cups frozen
  peas, defrosted
1 small bunch of mint,
  leaves chopped
finely grated zest of
  1 lemon
2 tbsp extra virgin olive
  oil
sea salt and freshly
  ground black pepper

Salmon is a wonderfully healthy fish due to the beneficial omega fatty acids it contains (good for your memory and lowering cholesterol and blood pressure). Adding a crunchy seeded topping to the salmon will give you an even bigger dose of omegas. The wasabi paste used to stick the seeds on top of the fish provides a nice kick. If you are not a wasabi fan then you can always use some pesto, tomato purée/paste or tapenade (olive paste).

To prepare the salmon, put the seeds in a shallow bowl and mix together with a good pinch of salt. Lightly spread the wasabi paste over the top of the salmon fillets, then gently press into the seeds, coating the top of each salmon fillet.

Heat a non-stick frying pan over a medium-high heat. Add a trickle of oil and fry the salmon, skin side down, for 4–5 minutes until the skin is crisp. Turn the fillets over and cook for 2 minutes until the seeds are golden and the salmon is just cooked through.

Meanwhile, put the stock and garlic in a medium-large saucepan over a high heat. Bring to the boil, then reduce the heat to medium-low and simmer for 1 minute until the garlic is softened. Add the peas and return to a simmer. Cook for 1–2 minutes until the peas are heated through.

Remove the pan from the heat and stir in the mint, lemon zest and extra virgin olive oil, then season with salt and pepper. Using a potato masher, crush the peas until they are fairly mushed up, but still retain some texture. Serve with the seed-crusted salmon and lemon wedges to squeeze over.

salmon burgers with pickled radish and wasabi mayo

SERVES 4

preparation time: 20 minutes, plus 30 minutes pickling

cooking time: 8 minutes

600g/1lb 5oz skinless salmon fillet, roughly chopped

finely grated zest of 1 lime

4 spring onions/ scallions, chopped

2.5cm/1in piece of root ginger, peeled and grated

1 egg, lightly beaten

1½ tbsp coconut or olive oil

4 burger buns or bread rolls, lightly toasted

4 handfuls of rocket/ arugula or lettuce

sea salt

For the pickled radish:

100ml/3½fl oz/scant ½ cup rice vinegar or white wine vinegar

2 tbsp honey

1 lime leaf, fresh or dried, torn into a few pieces (optional)

250g/9oz radishes, finely sliced

75g/2½oz sushi ginger, drained and roughly chopped

For the wasabi mayonnaise:

3 tbsp low-fat mayonnaise

3 tbsp low-fat crème fraîche

1 tsp wasabi paste, or more, to taste

If you love a good burger like me, but feel guilty having devoured one, you'll love this recipe as it's a lot better for you and comes with no reduction in taste satisfaction.

To make the pickled radish, put the vinegar, honey and lime leaf in a small saucepan over a medium heat to warm, stirring until the honey has dissolved, then remove from the heat. Leave to cool for 5 minutes, then stir in the radishes. Leave to pickle for about 30 minutes.

To make the salmon burgers, put the fish in a food processor with the lime zest, spring onions/scallions, grated ginger and egg. Season with salt and pulse until everything is just combined. Using your hands, shape into 4 burgers and transfer to a plate. Cover and chill until needed.

To make the mayonnaise, simply mix everything together and add more wasabi for a hotter flavour, if you like. Chill until needed.

When you are ready to serve, heat a frying pan over a medium heat. Add the oil and fry the burgers for 3–4 minutes on each side until lightly golden and only just firm to touch.

Drain the radishes from the pickling liquid, remove the lime leaf and stir in the sushi ginger.

To assemble the burgers, I prefer to spread the wasabi mayonnaise on both the bottom and top halves of the buns. Layer the bases with some rocket/ arugula, the burgers and some pickled radish, then top with the lids. Of course, it's entirely up to you how you choose to serve them. You may even prefer to serve open-topped burgers, using just the bottoms of the buns. Either way, I'm sure you'll find them delicious.

miso tuna with pickled vegetable salad and nori noodles

4 tuna steaks, about
150g/5½oz each
2 tbsp white miso paste
1 tbsp soy sauce
1 tbsp honey
1 tsp rice vinegar
rapeseed/canola oil, for
brushing

For the pickled vegetable salad:
125ml/4fl oz/½ cup rice
vinegar
2½ tbsp caster/
granulated sugar
½ cucumber, deseeded
and finely sliced
100g/3½oz radishes,
finely sliced
3 shallots, finely sliced
into rings
1 small fennel bulb, core
removed and very finely
sliced

For the noodles:
1 nori sheet or 2 tbsp
nori sprinkles
200g/7oz flat rice
noodles
2 tsp toasted sesame oil
1 tbsp toasted sesame or
black sesame seeds

This Japanese-inspired dish is super on many levels, not to mention super-duper healthy. If you can, try and plan ahead when making this, as the tuna will certainly benefit from marinating overnight to really take on the flavours of the marinade. Plus, if you make the pickled vegetable salad at the same time, the veggies will taste amazing as the pickling liquor becomes more mellow and slightly less acidic over time.

First, put the tuna in a shallow non-reactive bowl. Mix together the miso, soy sauce, honey and rice vinegar using a small whisk until you have a smooth paste. Pour over the tuna and turn the fish over to completely coat in the miso marinade. Cover and leave to marinate in the refrigerator for at least 1 hour, but overnight would be preferable.

Meanwhile, pickle the vegetables. Heat the rice vinegar and sugar in a saucepan over a low heat until the sugar dissolves. Leave to cool. Put the cucumber, radishes, shallots and fennel in a large non-reactive bowl, then pour over the cooled vinegar. Mix well and leave the vegetables to 'pickle' while the tuna is marinating, stirring occasionally.

If you are using a nori sheet, tear into small pieces and put in a blender. Whizz to fine sprinkles.

When you are ready to serve, heat a large frying pan or griddle/grill pan over a medium-high heat. Remove the tuna from the marinade, lightly wiping off any excess with your fingers. Brush a little oil on the surface of the pan and cook the tuna for 3 minutes on each side until it is caramelized around the edges and is almost cooked through. If the marinade appears to be burning too quickly, reduce the heat.

Meanwhile, cook the rice noodles according to the packet instructions. Drain well and toss with the sesame oil, sesame seeds and the nori sprinkles. Serve with the pickled vegetable salad and tuna.

pan-fried mackerel with wheat berry salad

4–8 mackerel fillets, depending on their size
a squeeze of lemon juice

For the salad:
4 raw beetroot/beets, cut into bite-size wedges
1 butternut squash, peeled and cut into small bite-size chunks
2 tbsp olive oil, plus extra for frying
150g/5½oz/1 cup wheat berries, soaked in water overnight
1 bay leaf
1 large radicchio, roughly chopped, or 50g/1¾oz baby ruby chard
1 small red onion, finely sliced
1 small bunch of parsley, chopped
sea salt and freshly ground black pepper

For the honey and mustard dressing:
4 tbsp rapeseed/canola oil
2 tbsp honey
2 tbsp white wine vinegar
1 tbsp wholegrain mustard
finely grated zest of 1 orange

Wheat berries are a versatile whole grain with a sweet, nutty taste and a delightful chewy texture, which are packed with fibre, antioxidants and disease-fighting compounds called lignans. They are becoming more widely available in supermarkets – if you can't locate them, great alternatives are farro, pearl barley, pearled spelt or bulgur wheat, which is in fact precooked, dried and cracked wheat berries.

Preheat the oven to 200°C/400°F/gas 6. Put the beetroot/beets and squash in a roasting pan and toss in the olive oil. Season with salt and pepper, then roast for about 45 minutes until softened and turning golden. Remove from the oven and leave to cool to room temperature.

Meanwhile, put the wheat berries in a medium-large saucepan, cover with plenty of water and add a pinch of salt. Add the bay leaf and bring to the boil over a high heat, then reduce the heat to medium and simmer for 25 minutes, or until the wheat berries are tender. Drain and remove the bay leaf.

To make the dressing, put all of the ingredients in a screw-topped jar, seal, then shake well and leave to one side.

Toss together the wheat berries, roasted beetroot/beets and squash, radicchio, red onion and parsley. Pour over the dressing and gently mix together.

To cook the mackerel, heat a trickle of olive oil in a frying pan over a high heat. Season the mackerel with salt and pepper and fry for 2–3 minutes on each side until golden. For even cooking, lightly press the fillets down into the pan using the base of a fish slice as they cook. Squeeze over the lemon juice and serve with the wheat berry salad.

preparation time: 20 minutes
cooking time: 30 minutes

baked mackerel with orange and fennel salad

4 whole fresh mackerel,
 gutted and cleaned,
 about 300g/10½oz
 each
olive oil, for rubbing
sea salt and freshly
 ground black pepper

For the orange and fennel salad:
500g/1lb 2oz new
 potatoes
2 large oranges
1 fennel bulb
100g/3½oz/2 cups baby
 spinach leaves
1 small red onion, finely
 sliced
1 large ripe avocado,
 peeled, pitted and
 sliced
2½ tbsp pumpkin seeds

*For the orange and mustard
 dressing:*
2 tbsp Dijon mustard
2 tbsp walnut or olive oil
2 tsp honey

Mackerel is a super-healthy fish to cook because it contains more omega-3 fatty acids than any other fish (excellent for brainpower and lowering your cholesterol levels). It's also pretty economical, too. As it's a seasonal fish, you may not always be able to get hold of fresh mackerel, so serve this refreshing salad with equally healthy smoked mackerel instead.

Cook the potatoes for 15 minutes in a pan of boiling salted water until tender. Drain and leave to cool.

Preheat the oven to 180°C/350°F/gas 4 and line a baking pan with foil.

Cut the top and bottom off the oranges, then put them flat on a board. Following the curve of the oranges, cut away the peel and pith using a sharp knife. Retain the peel. Hold each orange over a bowl to catch the juices and cut out the segments, leaving behind the membrane between them. Squeeze any juice out of the remaining part of the oranges into the juice bowl. Leave the orange segments and juice to one side.

Make 3 slashes on both sides of each mackerel and put in the prepared baking pan. Rub a little olive oil, salt and pepper into the skin of each fish, then put a piece or two of the orange peel inside each one. Bake for 12–15 minutes, or until the fish is cooked through. A good way to check is to see if the top dorsal fin comes out easily. If it doesn't, return to the oven for a few more minutes to carry on cooking.

To assemble the salad, slice the fennel in half, cut out and discard the tough central core and very thinly slice the fennel. Keep some of the fennel fronds, if there are any, to add to the salad. Cut the cooled potatoes into slices or slim wedges, then gently mix with the spinach leaves, red onion, avocado, orange segments and fennel. Scatter with the pumpkin seeds and fennel fronds, if using.

To make the dressing, simply mix everything together, adding 4 tablespoons of the reserved orange juice, and season with salt and pepper. Pour over the salad and lightly toss together. Serve the baked mackerel with the salad.

spaghetti with sardines and spinach

3 tbsp pine nuts

200g/7oz whole-wheat
  spaghetti

120g/4¼oz canned
  sardines in olive oil

2 garlic cloves, chopped

1 red chilli, deseeded and
  finely chopped

25g/1oz/heaped ¼ cup
  sultanas/golden raisins

2 tbsp small capers

100g/3½oz/2 cups baby
  spinach leaves, roughly
  chopped

juice and finely grated
  zest of ½ lemon

sea salt and freshly
  ground black pepper

extra virgin olive oil,
  for drizzling

Next time you think you've nothing in for a dinner for two, take a look in your cupboard and you may well see a can of sardines waiting to be used up. These little silvery fish shouldn't be overlooked as they are a super-concentrated source of omega-3 fatty acids and vitamins B12 and D. They have a meaty texture and rich flavour, which means a little goes a long way. A pasta dish like this is easier to cook in smaller portions as you want to be able to toss the spaghetti in the pan with all of the other ingredients. If you overfill the pan it's just too hard to mix together.

Heat a frying pan over a medium heat and toast the pine nuts for a few minutes, stirring occasionally, until they are light golden. Remove from the pan and leave to cool.

Cook the spaghetti in a pan of boiling salted water for 10 minutes, or until al dente.

Meanwhile, heat a large frying pan over a medium-low heat. Pour the oil from the sardines into the pan and gently fry the garlic and chilli for about 1 minute until softened but not golden.

Increase the heat to high, tip the sardines into the pan and roughly break up with a wooden spoon. Fry for a minute or so to heat through. Add the sultanas/golden raisins, capers and toasted pine nuts. Fry for a further 30 seconds, then add a ladle of the pasta cooking water and the spinach and lemon zest. Toss together to wilt the spinach.

Add in the cooked pasta, season with salt and pepper and toss everything together over the heat until completely combined. Divide onto plates or into bowls and scatter over the lemon zest. Serve with a drizzle of extra virgin olive oil.

PS... If you are cooking for one, any of the leftovers are really nice served cold the next day as a salad. Add a fresh squeeze of lemon juice and a drizzle of oil and you're away. A few added halved cherry tomatoes work pretty well, too.

preparation time: 10 minutes
cooking time: 40 minutes

prawn and brown rice jambalaya

2 tbsp olive oil
1 onion, finely chopped
3 celery stalks, finely
   chopped
1 yellow or red pepper,
   deseeded and diced
4 garlic cloves, crushed
1 bay leaf
1 tsp smoked paprika
a pinch of cayenne
   pepper
200g/7oz/1 cup brown
   rice
400g/14oz canned
   chopped tomatoes
400g/14oz canned red
   kidney beans, drained
750ml/26fl oz/3 cups
   chicken or vegetable
   stock
400g/14oz raw, peeled
   king prawns/jumbo
   shrimp
1 small handful of
   chopped parsley
sea salt and freshly
   ground black pepper

To serve:
4 spring onions/
   scallions, finely
   chopped
lemon wedges

I've adapted a classic Creole rice dish in a couple of ways to give it a healthy boost, but you still get to enjoy the beautiful mix of strong flavours and great textures the traditional dish is known for. Jambalaya is French for 'mixed up' or 'jumbled' – rice, spices, vegetables, meats and seafood are all cooked together in one pot. I have used prawns/shrimp, a great antioxidant, and fibre-rich kidney beans, plus nutty brown rice for even more goodness. Serve with chopped spring onions/scallions and fresh lemon juice to really liven things up.

Heat the oil in a large heavy-based frying pan or a wide flameproof casserole over a medium-high heat. Fry the onion, celery, yellow or red pepper and garlic for 5–8 minutes until softened. Stir in the bay leaf, paprika, cayenne pepper and rice and cook for a further minute or so.

Add the chopped tomatoes, kidney beans and stock to the pan. Bring to a simmer, then cover with a lid, reduce the heat to low and cook for about 25 minutes, until the rice is almost tender.

Season the prawns/shrimp and stir into the pan. Cook for about 5 minutes until the prawns/shrimp turn pink. Stir in the parsley and season with salt and pepper. Scatter with spring onions/scallions and serve with lemon wedges to squeeze over.

PS... If you want to make this into a chicken jambalaya, the prawns/shrimp can be substituted with 2 chicken breast fillets, cut into strips. Add to the pan when the onion, celery and pepper have softened, frying for a couple of minutes before continuing with the recipe.

SERVES 4

preparation time: 15 minutes,
plus 10 minutes soaking
cooking time: 15 minutes

harissa prawns and cavolo nero with saffron couscous

1 large pinch of saffron
strands
2 tbsp flaked/sliced
almonds or pine nuts
225g/8oz/1⅓ cups
whole-wheat couscous
75g/2½oz/scant ⅔ cup
sultanas/golden raisins
2 tbsp olive oil
375ml/13fl oz/1½ cups
hot vegetable or fish
stock
1 large red onion, finely
sliced
400g/14oz raw, shell-on
or peeled king prawns/
jumbo shrimp
2 tsp harissa paste
250g/9oz cavolo nero,
central core removed
and leaves roughly
chopped
1 preserved lemon,
deseeded and finely
chopped
a squeeze of lemon juice
sea salt and freshly
ground black pepper

There is a very Middle Eastern feel to this dish, which is aromatic, fragrant and spicy. It is an ideal recipe to make when you need something on the table quickly and, providing you have a fairly well-stocked larder, you shouldn't need to do much shopping either. Defrosted frozen prawns/shrimp work well, as do any other greens instead of cavolo nero (also known as black cabbage or Tuscan Kale).

Put the saffron strands in a small bowl and add 1 tablespoon water. Leave to soak for 10 minutes.

Meanwhile, heat a frying pan over a medium heat and toast the almonds for a few minutes, stirring occasionally, until they are light golden. Remove from the pan and leave to cool.

Put the couscous and sultanas/golden raisins in a large bowl. Stir the soaked saffron and half the olive oil into the stock, then pour over the couscous. Stir and cover with a plate or cling film/plastic wrap. Leave to stand for about 5 minutes until the couscous has absorbed the stock. Run a fork through to separate the grains. Cover and keep warm.

Heat the remaining olive oil in a large frying pan or wok over a medium-high heat. Add the onion and fry for about 5 minutes until golden. Add the prawns/shrimp and fry until they just turn pink, then stir in the harissa paste and toss around in the pan to coat the prawns/shrimp.

Add half of the cavolo nero and toss to mix with the prawns, then add the remaining cabbage. Stir-fry for 5 minutes, adding a couple of tablespoons of water to the pan to create some steam, which will cook the cavolo nero. When it is tender, season with salt and pepper and mix in the chopped preserved lemon.

Transfer the couscous to a serving bowl and spoon over the prawns/shrimp and cavolo nero. Add a squeeze of lemon juice and serve scattered with the toasted almonds.

pad thai with prawns and plenty of veggies

200g/7oz flat rice
  noodles
2 tbsp fish sauce
1½ tbsp soft brown sugar
2 tbsp rice vinegar
¼–½ tsp dried chilli/hot
  pepper flakes
1½ tbsp rapeseed/canola
  oil
3 garlic cloves, crushed
1 small red pepper,
  deseeded and finely
  sliced
150g/5½oz/1¼ cups
  frozen edamame beans
  (green soybeans),
  defrosted
150g/5½oz mange tout/
  snow peas, thinly sliced
  into strips
300g/10½oz large raw,
  peeled prawns/shrimp
2 eggs, lightly beaten
200g/7oz/3½ cups bean
  sprouts
1 bunch of spring
  onions/scallions, finely
  sliced

To serve:
50g/1¾oz/⅓ cup
  unsalted roasted
  peanuts, chopped
lime wedges

I've given a healthier twist to this delicious Thai noodle dish by including more fresh vegetables than usual and cutting down on the rice noodles. Yet despite these modifications it is still bursting with the classic Pad Thai flavour – spicy, sour, sweet and salty. You can easily swap the prawns/shrimp with some chicken breast or firm tofu to ring the changes. If you don't have a very big wok, this is best made in two batches so the wok doesn't become overcrowded. If you cook too much in one go, everything can become a little soggy. My best advice is to have everything completely prepared and ready to cook, so whether you cook in one or two batches it is nice, simple and stress free to make.

Cook the rice noodles according to the packet instructions. Drain and refresh under cold running water. Leave to one side.

Mix together the fish sauce, sugar, rice vinegar, chilli/hot pepper flakes and 1 tablespoon water in a non-reactive bowl. Leave to one side.

Heat a wok over a high heat and add the oil. When the oil is hot, add the garlic, red pepper, edamame and mange tout/snow peas and stir-fry for a minute to soften the vegetables slightly. Add the prawns/shrimp and fry until they turn pink, then add the noodles and stir continuously for 30 seconds.

Push the noodles to one side of the wok and pour the eggs into the other side. Leave to cook for about 30 seconds, then combine with the noodles, prawns/shrimp and vegetables.

Stir in the fish sauce mixture, bean sprouts and spring onions/scallions. Stir-fry for a minute or so until the bean sprouts are cooked. Serve scattered with the peanuts, with lime wedges to squeeze over.

preparation time: 15 minutes

cooking time: 35 minutes

cauliflower curry with fresh mango pickle

2 tbsp coconut oil

1 tbsp brown mustard
   seeds

1 onion, finely chopped

6 garlic cloves, crushed

3 tbsp Madras curry paste

1 tbsp tomato purée/paste

1 cauliflower, broken
   into bite-size florets

200g/7oz/heaped 1 cup
   red lentils

750ml/26fl oz/3 cups
   vegetable stock

150g/5½oz/3 cups baby
   spinach leaves

juice of ½ lemon

1 small bunch of
   coriander/cilantro,
   chopped

sea salt

cooked brown basmati
   rice, to serve (optional)

For the mango pickle:

2 tsp coconut oil

1 tsp brown mustard
   seeds

½ tsp nigella seeds

1 mango, peeled,
   pitted and diced into
   5–10mm/¼–½in cubes

1 tbsp white wine vinegar

1 tbsp caster/granulated
   sugar

¼ tsp chilli powder

Cauliflower often takes the supporting role as an accompaniment to curries but when partnered with fibre and protein-rich red lentils, it makes a well-balanced main course in its own right. The mango pickle is a fresh alternative to using high-sugar shop-bought mango chutney and also gives you a decent supply of vitamins C and A, too.

To make the curry, heat the oil in a large saucepan or wok. Add the mustard seeds and once they start to crackle and pop, add the onion and garlic. Fry together over a low heat for about 10 minutes until the onion is softened and lightly golden.

Stir in the curry paste and tomato purée/paste. Cook for 1 minute to release the spices in the paste, then stir in the cauliflower florets and lentils. Stir to coat in the paste, then pour in the stock. Bring to a simmer over a medium heat, then reduce the heat to low, cover with a lid and cook for 20 minutes until the cauliflower and lentils are tender.

Meanwhile, make the mango pickle. Heat the oil in a saucepan over a medium-low heat and add the mustard and nigella seeds. Cook for a couple of minutes until the seeds start popping. Add the remaining pickle ingredients and cook for 8 minutes until the mango is almost cooked through. Remove from the heat and leave to cool to room temperature.

Stir the spinach into the curry, a handful at a time, allowing it to wilt before adding more. Stir in the lemon juice, add the coriander/cilantro and season with salt.

Serve the curry with brown basmati rice, if you like, and the mango pickle.

*WASTE NOT, WANT NOT

Nigella seeds and brown mustard seeds are a great combination when paired together, such as in this simple carrot salad. Toss together 500g/1lb 2oz grated carrots, ½ finely sliced red onion, a handful of chopped coriander/ cilantro, the juice of ½ lemon and a good pinch of salt. Gently fry 2 teaspoons each of nigella and brown mustard seeds in 2 teaspoons of olive oil. Once they start to pop remove from the heat and stir into the carrot mixture.

rich vegetarian chilli with spiced walnut butter

SERVES 4–6

preparation time: 30 minutes
cooking time: 45 minutes

100g/3½oz/½ cup
  quinoa
2 tbsp coconut oil
1 onion, finely sliced
2 star anise
6 garlic cloves, crushed
1 green chilli, finely
  chopped
500–750ml/17–26fl oz/
  2–3 cups vegetable stock
100g/3½oz/heaped ½
  cup dried green lentils
100g/3½oz/heaped
  ½ cup bulgur wheat
400g/14oz canned red
  kidney beans, drained
2 tbsp tomato purée/paste
300ml/10½fl oz/
  1¼ cups red wine
400g/14oz canned
  chopped tomatoes
2 roasted red peppers,
  chopped
2 tsp cocoa powder
sea salt and freshly
  ground black pepper
lime wedges, to serve

For the spiced walnut butter:
200g/7oz/2 cups walnuts
2 tbsp coconut oil
1 tsp chilli powder
1½ tsp smoked paprika
1½ tsp ground cumin
2 tsp tomato ketchup
1 tsp yeast extract

For anyone who thinks a vegetarian chilli is boring and lacking in flavour, I challenge you to give this recipe a try. The highlight is the spiced walnut butter. I've taken inspiration from the fantastic Heston Blumenthal for this idea as he makes a similar version using traditional dairy butter. The walnut butter is far lower in saturated fat and much better for you. It adds a lovely smoky flavour and really enriches the consistency of the cooked chilli. Serve with rice, corn tortillas and lime wedges to squeeze over.

To make the spiced butter, put the walnuts in a food processor and blitz well until it forms a paste like thick peanut butter, scraping down the sides of the bowl every so often. Be patient with this, as it will start off looking crumbly, but will eventually become smooth and creamy.

Heat the coconut oil in a frying pan and lightly fry the chilli powder, smoked paprika and cumin for about 30–60 seconds. Remove from the heat and stir in the ketchup and yeast extract. Stir in the walnut paste and transfer to a bowl. Leave to one side.

To make the chilli, set a large saucepan over a medium heat and add the quinoa. Move around in the pan for a couple of minutes to toast the grains and bring out a nuttier flavour. Remove from the pan and leave to one side.

Heat the oil in the saucepan over a medium heat, then add the onion and star anise. Cook for about 5 minutes until the onion starts to soften and colour, then add the garlic and green chilli. Cook over a low heat for a further 5 minutes.

Stir in the toasted quinoa, 500ml/17fl oz/2 cups of the stock and all of the remaining chilli ingredients. Bring to a gentle boil, then reduce the heat to low and leave to simmer for 30 minutes, stirring occasionally, until you have a rich, thick chilli. Add any of the extra stock during cooking, if you feel it is required.

Stir in half of the spiced butter and remove the star anise (if you can locate them!). Season to taste with salt and pepper.

Serve with lime wedges and extra spiced walnut butter, for those who like a hotter chilli.

preparation time: 15 minutes
cooking time: 35 minutes

kale and bulgur wheat pilaf with roast figs

2 tbsp olive oil

2 onions, finely sliced

4 celery stalks, finely sliced

3 garlic cloves, crushed

1 bay leaf

¼ tsp ground allspice

300ml/10½fl oz/1¼ cups vegetable stock

150g/5½oz/scant 1 cup bulgur wheat

100g/3½oz/¾ cup blanched hazelnuts

300g/10½oz kale, stalks removed and shredded

½ tsp dried chilli/hot pepper flakes

finely grated zest of 1 orange

sea salt and freshly ground black pepper

4 tbsp Greek yogurt, to serve

For the figs:

8–12 figs, depending on their size

2 tbsp honey

125ml/4fl oz/½ cup freshly squeezed orange juice

1 tbsp white wine vinegar

Utterly delicious – I can't recommend this dish highly enough. It's bursting with colour, flavour and goodness.

Preheat the oven to 200°C/400°F/gas 6.

To make the pilaf, heat half the olive oil in a saucepan and add the onions. Cook over a gentle heat for about 10 minutes until the onions are golden brown. Add the celery, garlic, bay leaf and allspice. Continue to cook for a further 5 minutes.

Stir in the stock, add the bulgur wheat and bring to a simmer, then cover with a lid and cook over a low heat for 10 minutes. Remove from the heat, leaving the lid on, and leave to stand for about 10 minutes until the bulgur has absorbed the stock.

Meanwhile, cut each fig in half. Put the fig halves in a small roasting pan and drizzle the honey over the top. Pour over the orange juice and vinegar, then add some pepper. Roast for 20 minutes, basting with the juice a couple of times during cooking, until the figs are golden and a little sticky.

Put the hazelnuts in a small roasting pan and toast in the oven for 6–8 minutes until golden. Remove from the oven and, when cool enough to handle, roughly chop.

Just before the bulgur is ready, heat the remaining oil in a large frying pan or wok. Add the kale and chilli/hot pepper flakes and stir-fry for 2–3 minutes until just tender. If you feel it is burning, add a splash of water to create some steam in the pan. Season with salt and pepper, then remove from the heat.

Run a fork through the bulgur wheat and add to the kale. Toss around to mix together thoroughly, then scatter over the toasted hazelnuts and orange zest. Serve the pilaf with the roast figs, including any of their juices, and Greek yogurt.

kale is the new green

Kale, or curly kale, is one of the tastiest vegetables around, and without doubt deserves its title of being a superfood. Portion for portion it's hard to beat when it comes to the number of nutrients kale contains. For a vegetable, it's unbelievably high in calcium, plus it contains high levels of vitamins K, A and C, and antioxidants, folate, and is virtually fat free.

Kale has been cultivated for more than 2,000 years but until recently has been pretty much in the shadow of its relatives, cabbage, spinach and spring/collard greens. This robust vegetable has a delicious earthy, green and fresh flavour that can be used in many different ways from soups, stews, stir-fries and steamed to salads, juices and even crisps.

preparation

If kale leaves are small the stems will be nice and tender, so can be left attached to the leaf. However, bigger and older leaves tend to have tougher stalks so they are best removed by simply tearing the leaf away from either side of the stalk.

cooking

Kale has a relatively low moisture content and therefore doesn't shrink as much as most other greens (just think how much spinach shrinks when heated). Kale requires longer cooking, particularly older leaves. For delicious tender kale, simply steam, simmer in water or stock, or sauté in oil or butter for several minutes.

raw

Kale doesn't have to be cooked to be enjoyed. It can be used in juices, dips and salads. Younger more tender leaves are best although older leaves can be used and will benefit from a massage to tenderize them and give a sweeter flavour. Yes, you read right! To massage raw kale leaves you can rub/scrunch some olive oil, lemon juice and/or salt into the leaves for a few minutes until they feel tender. Enjoy alone or mixed into a salad.

recipe inspiration

Many recipes in this book contain kale, often with it featuring as a hero in the dish. It is very versatile and is used in lots of different ways in recipes as varied as Japanese Miso, Kale and Tofu Broth (see page 82), Kale Pesto Pasta with Crispy Prosciutto (see page 120), Middle Eastern Lamb with Kale and Prunes (see page 130) and Kale and Bulgur Wheat Pilaf with Roast Figs (see page 164). I love it so much, however, that I've a few more quick ideas I'd like to share.

kale crisps

These are available to buy pre-made now, with many different flavour variations, they are a fantastic healthy snack, but they are fun to make yourself, too. You can play around with all sorts of flavours to coat the leaves in or simply scatter them with salt.

My favourite is the savoury, slightly cheesy flavour of the following recipe – be warned, they are very moreish.

Preheat the oven to 100°C/200°F/gas ½. Wash and thoroughly dry 200g/7oz kale leaves, then remove the stalks and tear the leaves into large crisp-size pieces (they will shrink a little when baking). Mix together 1 tablespoon rapeseed/canola oil or melted coconut oil, 2 tablespoons tahini, 1 tablespoon yeast extract, ½ teaspoon dried chilli/hot pepper flakes and 1 tablespoon lemon juice in a large bowl. Add the kale and, using your hands, rub the dressing into all of the leaves. Don't worry about being quite rough, you need all the leaves coated. They are pretty robust. Transfer to two baking sheets lined with baking parchment. Spread evenly and bake for 30 minutes. Gently turn the leaves over and return to the oven for up to a further 30 minutes until they are completely dry and crisp. Do make sure they don't go brown on the edges, as this will taste bitter and burnt.

kale guacamole

As a stand alone recipe, guacamole can be a really healthy dip, but with the addition of kale it reaches another level, not to mention its super-green colour.

Put 1 handful of shredded young kale, 1 peeled garlic clove, 1 small diced red onion, 1 bunch of coriander/cilantro and a roughly chopped chilli into a food processor and blitz until fairly smooth. Transfer to a bowl and mix in 1 tablespoon extra virgin olive oil, 1 large mashed avocado and 1 deseeded and finely sliced tomato. Add lime juice, salt and pepper to taste.

chilli and soy kale

This has to be one of my favourite side dishes, not only with a juicy steak or piece of grilled/broiled fish, but also if I'm feeling a bit peckish and want something with a satisfying kick. It also makes a simple lunch that you can throw together in minutes. Serves 1.

Heat 1 tablespoon coconut oil in a wok over a medium heat. Stir-fry 1 chopped clove of garlic, 1 teaspoon sesame seeds and 1 finely sliced red chilli for about 30 seconds. Increase the heat and add 2 handfuls of shredded young kale. Toss around in the pan for a minute or so (longer if you prefer more cooked kale). Add a splash of soy and squeeze of lemon or lime juice. Toss to combine and serve.

kale superjuice

For an energizing boost to your day, you really must give this a try. It's very green, full of goodness and tastes so much nicer than you might expect it to! Serves 1.

Blitz 1 handful of kale leaves (tough stalks removed), 200ml/7fl oz/scant 1 cup fresh apple juice, 1 sprig of mint, 1 cucumber, 1cm/½in piece of root ginger, peeled, and a squeeze of lemon juice together in a blender for a couple of minutes until thoroughly blended. Serve and feel great.

portobello mushrooms with pomegranate couscous

SERVES 4

preparation time: 20 minutes

cooking time: 25 minutes

4–8 portobello
  mushrooms, depending
  on their size
4 tbsp pomegranate
  molasses
2 garlic cloves, crushed
2 tbsp olive oil
100ml/3½fl oz/scant
  ½ cup red wine
½ tsp dried chilli/hot
  pepper flakes
sea salt and freshly
  ground black pepper

For the couscous:
1 tbsp olive oil
1 tsp grated root ginger
1 garlic clove, crushed
4 carrots, peeled and
  coarsely grated
275ml/9½fl oz/scant 1¼
  cups hot vegetable stock
175g/6oz/1 cup whole-
  wheat couscous
1 small bunch of mint,
  leaves chopped
finely grated zest of
  ½ lemon
seeds from 1
  pomegranate, or
  100g/3½oz ready-
  prepared pomegranate
  seeds

Portobello mushrooms are a great substitute for meat if you don't eat meat, are trying to cut down on your red meat intake or simply fancy a vegetarian meal. They are naturally fat free, packed with goodness and great at retaining their nutrients when cooked.

Preheat the oven to 200°C/400°F/gas 6.

Put the mushrooms in a small roasting pan, stalks facing upwards. Mix together the pomegranate molasses, garlic, olive oil, red wine and chilli/hot pepper flakes. Pour over the mushrooms and rub into the gills. Season with salt and pepper and roast for 25 minutes until tender, turning halfway through.

Meanwhile, make the couscous. Heat a large saucepan over medium–low heat and add the oil. Gently sauté the ginger and garlic for 1 minute, then add the grated carrots. Stir around in the pan for a couple of minutes to soften slightly, then add the stock. Bring to a simmer, stir in the couscous, then remove from the heat. Cover with a lid and leave to stand for 5 minutes until the couscous has absorbed the stock.

Run a fork through the couscous to separate the grains, then stir in the mint, lemon zest and pomegranate seeds.

Serve the mushrooms whole or thickly sliced, spooning over any juices in the roasting pan, with the pomegranate couscous.

beetroot gnocchi with nutty watercress pesto

SERVES 4
(or 6 as a first course)
preparation time: 40 minutes
cooking time: about 1 hour

1 large raw beetroot/beet,
   about 200g/7oz
2 tbsp red or white wine
   vinegar
1kg/2lb 4oz Maris Piper
   potatoes, peeled and
   quartered
2 egg yolks
60g/2¼oz/⅔ cup finely
   grated Parmesan cheese,
   plus Parmesan shavings
   to serve
100–200g/3½–7oz/
   ¾–1½ cups wholemeal/
   whole-wheat flour, plus
   extra for dusting
extra virgin olive oil,
   for drizzling
75g/2½oz/¾ cup
   walnuts, lightly toasted,
   to serve

For the pesto:
85g/3oz/2 cups watercress
1 garlic clove
40g/1½oz/scant ½ cup
   walnuts
25g/1oz/¼ cup grated
   Parmesan cheese
a squeeze of lemon juice
80ml/2½fl oz/⅓ cup
   avocado or extra virgin
   olive oil
sea salt and freshly
   ground black pepper

Gnocchi might not be the sort of thing you usually make from scratch but believe me – this recipe is well worth it. Not only does it look amazing but also the beetroot flavour works brilliantly, especially when served with the vibrant green homemade pesto.

To make the pesto, put the watercress and garlic in a food processor and blend until roughly chopped. Add the walnuts, Parmesan, lemon juice and olive oil and blend to a relatively smooth consistency. Add a little water if it seems a little too thick. Season with salt and pepper. Spoon into a bowl and leave to one side.

Put the beetroot/beet and vinegar in a pan and cover with water. Bring to the boil, then simmer over a medium heat for 45–60 minutes, or until the beetroot/beet is completely tender. Remove from the heat, peel off the skin and roughly chop. Blend to a smooth purée in a food processor.

Cook the potatoes in a steamer set over boiling water for 15–20 minutes until tender. Press through a potato ricer into a large mixing bowl or mash until very smooth. Add 4 tablespoons of the beetroot/beet purée to the potato, along with the egg yolks, Parmesan, pepper and a good pinch of salt. Mix well, then gradually mix in the flour until the mixture starts to hold together without being too sticky. To test, gently press the dough with your finger. When it springs back, you won't need to add any more flour.

Divide the dough into 4 portions. Take a portion of the mixture and roll into a long sausage shape, about 3cm/1¼in thick, on a lightly floured surface. Cut into chunky nuggets using a floured knife. Repeat with the remaining portions of dough.

Bring a large pan of salted water to the boil over medium heat. Drop in the gnocchi and cook until they rise to the surface (about 2 minutes). Try not to overcrowd the pan – it may be best to cook them in a few batches.

When cooked, drain the gnocchi in a colander and toss in a little extra virgin olive oil. Transfer to a serving plate and spoon over the pesto. Scatter with the toasted walnuts, a twist of black pepper and shavings of Parmesan cheese, and serve on their own or with salad leaves, if you like.

roast ratatouille penne bake with crunchy seeds

1 large courgette/zucchini
1 aubergine/eggplant
1 red pepper
1 yellow pepper
1 red onion
400g/14oz ripe plum
  tomatoes, quartered
3 tbsp olive oil, plus extra
  for rubbing
a good pinch of saffron
  strands
1 bulb of garlic
300–400g/10½–14oz
  penne pasta (any type
  is fine – whole-wheat,
  spelt, gluten-free, etc.)
2 tbsp balsamic vinegar
1 bunch of basil, chopped
sea salt and freshly
  ground black pepper

For the topping:
50g/1¾oz/½ cup grated
  Parmesan cheese
6 tbsp mixed seeds,
  including sunflower,
  pumpkin, linseed/
  flaxseed, chia and hemp
3 tbsp pine nuts
2 tsp crushed coriander
  seeds
2 tbsp olive oil

Ratatouille is such a simple way of getting plenty of veg into your diet and roasting them in a large pan means you can cook plenty at one time. It makes a great side dish but to serve as a main meal I like to toss the ratatouille into pasta and bake in the oven, topped with a super-healthy mix of seeds and Parmesan. You can buy mixed bags of seeds, which are perfect for this recipe and can save you the cost of having to buy individual bags.

Preheat the oven to 200°C/400°F/gas 6.

Cut the courgette/zucchini, aubergine/eggplant, peppers and onion into 1–2cm/½–¾in chunks. Put in a large roasting pan with the tomatoes and toss in the olive oil, saffron strands, salt and pepper.

Rub the whole garlic bulb with a drop of olive oil and wrap in a piece of foil. Put the roasting pan and the garlic in the oven and roast for 45 minutes, turning the vegetables just once during cooking.

Meanwhile, cook the pasta in a saucepan of boiling water, according to the packet instructions, until al dente, then drain and return to the pan.

Remove the garlic and ratatouille from the oven. Unwrap the garlic and cut off the top. Squeeze out the creamy roasted garlic and toss into the cooked pasta with the balsamic vinegar and basil. Transfer to the roasting pan and mix with the ratatouille.

Mix all the topping ingredients together and scatter over the top of the ratatouille and pasta. Alternatively, transfer to a clean oven-to-table dish, if you intend on serving the dish at the table.

Return the ratatouille to the oven and bake for 10 minutes until the seeds are golden and crisp.

MAKES 2 LARGE
OR 4 SMALL
preparation time: 35 minutes,
plus 1 hour proving
cooking time: 25 minutes

spelt and hemp pizzas

Spelt is a wheat-based grain that's far lower in gluten than most other wheat flours. The addition of shelled hemp seeds really makes these pizzas stand out. They're wonderfully high in omega fatty acids, protein, iron and magnesium, and add a rich nutty flavour and texture to the pizza bases. Top the pizzas with your favourite toppings or do as I have and use artichokes, ricotta and olives.

For the bases:
300g/10½oz/2¼ cups wholegrain spelt flour, plus extra for dusting
75g/2½oz/scant ½ cup shelled hemp seeds
2 tsp fast-action/instant active dried yeast
1 tsp salt
50ml/1¾fl oz/3½ tbsp rapeseed/canola, olive or hemp oil, plus extra for greasing, rubbing and drizzling

For the tomato sauce:
2 tbsp olive oil
1 onion, finely chopped
2 garlic cloves, crushed
500g/1lb 2oz ripe tomatoes, deseeded and diced
1 tbsp fresh or 1 tsp dried oregano
sea salt and freshly ground black pepper

For the topping:
200g/7oz ricotta cheese
400g/14oz canned artichokes, drained and quartered
1 handful of pitted black olives
1 handful of oregano leaves

To make the base dough, mix together the flour, hemp seeds, yeast and salt in large bowl and make a well in the middle. Pour in 200ml/7fl oz/ scant 1 cup warm water and the oil, then bring together with a wooden spoon, or using your hands, until you have a soft and fairly wet dough. Add up to 50ml/1¾fl oz/3½ tablespoons more warm water if the dough feels too dry or it is not coming together properly. Turn out onto a flour-dusted surface. Knead for about 10 minutes until smooth and elastic. Alternatively, you can mix everything together in a food mixer with a dough hook for about 5 minutes.

Put the dough in a clean, lightly oiled bowl and cover with a piece of oiled cling film/plastic wrap. Leave to rise in a warm place for about 30 minutes, or until it has doubled in size.

Meanwhile, to make the tomato sauce, heat the olive oil in a saucepan over a medium-low heat and add the onion. Sauté for 10 minutes, or until softened. Stir in the garlic, tomatoes and oregano. Increase the heat to medium and bring to a simmer, then cook for 10 minutes until the sauce is a thick, rich consistency. Season to taste with salt and pepper.

Divide the dough into half or quarters, depending on how many pizzas you wish to make, and roll into balls. Rub each ball all over with a little oil and put on an oiled baking sheet. Re-cover with the oiled cling film/plastic wrap and leave to rise in a warm place for a further 30 minutes.

Preheat the oven to 240°C/475°F/gas 8.

Roll the risen dough into rough circles and transfer to baking sheets lined with baking parchment. Spread the tomato sauce over the top and add some ricotta, artichokes, olives and oregano. Drizzle with olive oil and bake for 8–10 minutes until golden. Serve hot.

SERVES 4

preparation time: 10 minutes,
plus cooling
cooking time: 15 minutes

feta, pea and mint quinoa salad

200g/7oz/heaped 1 cup
  quinoa
150g/5½oz/1 cup frozen
  peas, defrosted
200g/7oz/1½ cups
  crumbled feta cheese
1 bunch of mint, leaves
  chopped
100g/3½oz/¾ cup pitted
  green olives, roughly
  chopped
55g/2oz/1½ cups rocket/
  arugula or baby spinach
  leaves, roughly chopped
juice and grated zest of
  1 lemon
2 tbsp extra virgin olive
  oil
sea salt and freshly
  ground black pepper

The combination of feta cheese, peas and mint has been a favourite of mine for a long time now, although I'd usually mix them with pasta. Quinoa makes a great substitute when I am in the mood for something a bit lighter and lower on the carbs. It's well worth making enough of this salad so you have plenty of leftovers for the next day as it makes a great packed lunch to take to work, or a side dish to serve with some roast chicken or grilled fish.

Put the quinoa in a saucepan with 500ml/17fl oz/2 cups water. Set over a high heat and bring to the boil, then cook at a rolling boil for 1 minute. Cover with a lid, reduce the heat to low and leave to cook for 12 minutes. Remove from the heat, leaving the lid on, and leave to stand for a further 5 minutes. Run a fork through to separate the grains. Leave to cool.

When the quinoa is cool, toss together with all of the remaining ingredients. Season with salt and pepper before serving.

pearl barley and mushroom risotto with goats' cheese

15g/½oz dried porcini mushrooms

4 tbsp olive or rapeseed/ canola oil

400g/14oz mixed wild and chestnut/cremini mushrooms, sliced

2 leeks, finely sliced

4 garlic cloves, crushed

1 tbsp thyme leaves, plus extra to serve

300g/10½oz/1½ cups pearl barley

250ml/9fl oz/1 cup white wine or vermouth

750ml/26fl oz/3 cups hot vegetable stock

125g/4½oz soft spreadable goats' cheese

125g/4½oz firm goats' cheese log, rind removed and diced into pieces

sea salt and freshly ground black pepper

Using pearl barley as a substitute for risotto rice gives a slightly different texture to a risotto and really increases its nutritional value, mainly in the form of fibre. It does take slightly longer to cook than rice but the bonus is that you don't have to keep stirring as it cooks.

Using a pair of scissors, snip the dried porcini into small pieces and put in a jug. Pour over 250ml/9fl oz/1 cup boiling water. Leave to soak for 20 minutes.

Heat half the oil in a large saucepan over a medium heat. Add about two-thirds of the fresh mushrooms, the leeks, garlic and thyme and sauté for 5 minutes until the leeks and mushrooms are softened.

Add the pearl barley and cook for 1 minute. Pour in the wine and continue to cook, stirring, until it is absorbed.

Add the porcini mushrooms and their soaking liquid to the saucepan, then stir in two-thirds of the hot stock. Bring to a simmer over a low heat and leave to cook for about 30–40 minutes until the barley is tender, stirring occasionally and topping up with the remaining stock if it looks dry.

Meanwhile, heat the remaining oil in a frying pan over a high heat. Add the remaining fresh mushrooms and fry for 1 minute or so until they are golden all over. Season with salt and pepper.

When the risotto is cooked, remove the pan from the heat. Stir in the soft goats' cheese to give a creamy consistency and season with salt and pepper. Stir through the diced goats' cheese, then serve with the golden mushrooms and a few extra thyme leaves scattered over the top.

smoky roots tortilla with super-green salad

olive oil, for frying

2 onions, very finely sliced

700g/1lb 9oz peeled root vegetables, such as parsnip, swede/ rutabaga, sweet potato, potato and carrots, very finely sliced

6 eggs

2 tsp Spanish smoked paprika

sea salt and freshly ground black pepper

For the super-green salad:

150g/5½oz/4 cups finely shredded kale

100g/3½oz/2 cups baby spinach leaves

6 spring onions/ scallions, finely sliced

1 ripe avocado, peeled, pitted and diced

4 tbsp pumpkin seeds

juice of ½ lemon

2 tbsp avocado or extra virgin olive oil

Traditionally Spanish tortilla is made with potatoes, but I quite like using a combination of different root veg for the various flavours they offer, not to mention the fact that it is a pretty healthy way to use up any odds and ends in your refrigerator that you are not sure what to do with. The tortilla's smoky flavour comes from the Spanish smoked paprika, giving it a lovely, mellow spicy warmth as well as a nice colour. To make this a perfectly well-balanced meal, serve with the mouth-watering salad. It's full of superfoods that will make you feel great.

Pour enough olive oil into a large non-stick frying pan to cover the base about 5mm/¼in deep. Set over a medium heat and add the onions. Gently cook for about 10 minutes until they are softened.

Add the root vegetables to the pan and turn gently to coat in the oil and onions. Season with salt and pepper and cover with a lid. (If you don't have one big enough, you can put a baking sheet over the top of the frying pan.) Cook for 15–20 minutes until the vegetables are softened, turning occasionally, but making sure you don't break up the vegetables too much.

Transfer the vegetables to a large bowl and pour any of the excess oil back into the frying pan. Leave the veggies to cool for about 5 minutes.

Beat together the eggs and paprika, then add to the bowl with the vegetables. Stir briefly to coat the vegetables with egg and leave to stand for a further 5 minutes, allowing the eggs to become absorbed into the root vegetables.

Return the frying pan to a low heat. Season the egg mixture with salt and pepper and pour into the pan. Flatten the surface. Cook for 10 minutes, making sure the heat isn't too high, otherwise the base will burn.

Gently slide the tortilla onto a plate. Place another plate over the top, flip over and then slide the tortilla back into the frying pan, now with the uncooked side down. Continue to cook for a further 5 minutes until the edges feel firm but the middle still feels slightly soft.

While the tortilla is cooking, simply toss all of the salad ingredients together and season with salt and pepper.

Cut the tortilla into wedges and serve with the salad.

nutty green vegetable tart

For the tart base:

80ml/2½fl oz/⅓ cup
  rapeseed/canola or
  olive oil, plus extra for
  greasing
100g/3½oz/1 cup rolled
  oats
85g/3oz/scant 1 cup
  mixed nuts, such as
  almonds, walnuts,
  pecans and hazelnuts
150g/5½oz/scant 1¼
  cups wholemeal/whole-
  wheat flour, plus extra
  for dusting
1 egg, lightly beaten
2 sun-dried tomato
  halves, finely chopped
1 tsp thyme leaves

For the filling:

2 tbsp olive oil
3 garlic cloves, crushed
1 leek, finely sliced
1 courgette/zucchini,
  sliced
100g/3½oz/2 cups baby
  spinach leaves
100g/3½oz/⅔ cup
  frozen peas, defrosted
75g/2½oz/⅔ cup grated
  Gruyère cheese
3 eggs
125ml/4fl oz/½ cup
  almond milk (or cows
  milk, if preferred)
a good pinch of cayenne
  pepper
sea salt and freshly
  ground black pepper

I do quite like a tart or a quiche from time to time but feel unhealthy eating pastry bases as they are fairly high in saturated fat from all the butter they contain. So after having a play around in the kitchen, I decided to substitute the pastry with a lovely mix of oats, nuts and wholemeal/whole-wheat flour bound together with omega-rich rapeseed/canola oil and egg. It works perfectly. The filling is packed full of green vegetables, a little Gruyère cheese, eggs and almond milk, which carries on the nutty theme of the tart (although you can use any milk you like for this). It tastes delicious. Serve the tart cut into big wedges with a salad. Any leftover tart is great the next day for lunch.

Preheat the oven to 200°C/400°F/gas 6 and brush a 23cm/9in tart pan with a little oil.

Put the oats and nuts in a food processor and blitz until they form a coarse floury texture. Add the flour, egg, sun-dried tomatoes, thyme, olive oil and a good pinch of salt. Briefly blitz to form a soft dough. If it seems a bit dry, add a little cold water until you have the correct consistency.

Turn the dough out onto a lightly floured surface and roll out until it is big enough to line the base and sides of the prepared tart pan. Transfer to the pan. Don't worry if it breaks up, just press into the pan as evenly as you can, patching up any cracks. Trim the top edge to neaten off. Bake for 20 minutes, or until it is light golden brown and firm.

Meanwhile, heat the olive oil for the filling in a large frying pan over a medium heat. Add the garlic, leek and courgette/zucchini and sauté for 5–8 minutes until the vegetables have softened. Stir in the spinach until it has wilted, then add the peas. Season with salt and pepper. Transfer to the base of the tart and scatter over half of the cheese.

Put the tart pan on a baking sheet. Beat together the eggs and milk, and season with salt and cayenne pepper. Carefully pour over the top of the vegetables until the mixture reaches the top of the pastry. Scatter over the remaining cheese. Bake for 25 minutes, or until the egg is just set.

Serve warm or cold.

something
sweet

seared pineapple, brazil nut brittle and lime yogurt

SERVES 4

preparation time: 20 minutes
cooking time: 5 minutes

1 small to medium
  pineapple
6 tbsp low-fat plain
  yogurt
2cm/¾in piece of root
  ginger, peeled and
  very finely chopped or
  grated
1 handful of mint leaves,
  finely shredded
juice and zest of 1 lime

For the Brazil nut brittle:
55g/2oz/½ cup palm
  sugar or soft brown
  sugar
125g/4½oz/1 cup Brazil
  nuts, roughly chopped

Pimp up your fruit and serve some juicy pineapple in a far more interesting way than just on its own. Pineapple is a really good fruit to eat at the end of a meal as it is known for being great for the digestion, as well as being loaded full of vitamins C and A, fibre, calcium and potassium. The Brazil nut brittle that's served with the pineapple uses a higher nut to caramelized sugar ratio than usual. This allows the amazing goodness of Brazil nuts to outweigh the little bit of naughtiness coming from the sugar.

To make the brittle, put the sugar in a saucepan and set the pan over a medium-low heat. Allow the sugar to melt, swirling the pan very gently a couple of times, making sure the sugar doesn't burn around the edges before the rest has melted. When it has melted, add the Brazil nuts and mix around, coating them in the caramel. Immediately pour onto a non-stick baking sheet. Leave to cool for about 10 minutes.

With a sharp knife, cut the top and bottom off the pineapple, then slice off the skin. Halve the pineapple down the middle, then cut each half into 4, giving you 8 wedges. Slice off the inner core.

Heat a griddle/grill pan or large non-stick frying pan over a high heat. Place the pineapple wedges in the hot pan. Cook for 2–3 minutes on each side until the natural sugars have started to caramelize.

Meanwhile, mix together the yogurt, ginger, mint, lime zest and juice.

Serve the griddled pineapple with some of the yogurt spooned over. Break the Brazil nut brittle into smaller pieces and scatter over the top.

PS... Searing fruit is a great way to bring out its natural sweetness, especially if it's not completely ripe. You could also try using mango, banana, peaches or nectarines.

SERVES 4
preparation time: 5 minutes,
plus 2 hours soaking

strawberries with vanilla cashew cream

400g/14oz ripe
  strawberries
freshly ground black
  pepper
a few basil leaves, finely
  shredded (optional)

For the vanilla cashew cream:
150g/5½oz/1¼ cups
  cashew nuts
seeds from 1 vanilla
  pod/bean
2 tbsp maple syrup

The classic British combination of juicy strawberries served with an extravagant helping of cream is an utterly delicious mix and luckily if you're in the mood for being healthy you can still enjoy them together. 'How?', I hear you ask. Well, rather than using dairy cream that is high in saturated fat, you can serve strawberries with a very clever cream made from cashew nuts. It's genius. Of course, cashews do contain fats, but don't worry, they are the good fats that we need everyday. They are also rich in calcium and zinc, which are vital for your immune system and for healthy skin. Give this a try and you'll be amazed.

To make the cashew cream, put the cashews in a bowl and cover with water. Leave to soak for about 2 hours to soften.

Drain the softened cashews and put them in a food processor with 125ml/4fl oz/½ cup cold water. Blend until completely smooth, adding up to 125ml/4fl oz/½ cup more water, as necessary, until it is smooth and creamy, and you have a cream as thick or loose as you like. Add the vanilla seeds and maple syrup and briefly blitz to combine.

Prepare the strawberries as you like, whether you want to serve them whole or cut up. Add a twist of pepper and scatter over the basil, if using. Serve with the vanilla cashew cream.

＊ WHY NOT TRY...

Serving this layered up in sundae glasses.
You could even add some flaked/sliced almonds,
toasted oats or granola for extra crunch.

preparation time: 15 minutes,
plus cooling and chilling
cooking time: 15–25 minutes

green tea and mandarin poached pears

4 green tea bags

125g/4½oz/scant ⅔ cup
   golden caster/raw cane
   sugar

5cm/2in piece of root
   ginger, peeled and cut
   into thin slices

peeled zest from
   2 mandarins

4 firm pears, peeled,
   halved and cores
   removed

Greek yogurt, to serve
   (optional)

This is a really light dessert to end a meal and a very good way to use those pears that are under-ripe. Poaching them in a powerful antioxidant green tea, mandarin and ginger infusion will soften them up nicely and give them a great flavour. Serve alone or with a dollop of Greek yogurt for a creamier finish.

Put the tea bags in a jug with 1l/35fl oz/4 cups boiling water. Leave to brew for 5 minutes before discarding the tea bags. Pour the tea into a saucepan wide enough to hold the pears in a single layer.

Stir the sugar, ginger and mandarin zest into the tea. Put over a medium heat and stir until the sugar has dissolved. Add the pears in a single layer. Bring the liquid to a simmer and cover the pears with a circle of baking parchment to hold them in the liquid. Reduce the heat to medium-low and gently cook until the pears are tender. This could take between 10 and 20 minutes, depending on the pears and how ripe they are. Insert a skewer or tip of a sharp knife into each pear to check they are cooked and tender throughout.

Gently remove the pears with a slotted spoon, transfer to a plate or tray and leave to cool.

Return the poaching liquid to the heat and boil until it has reduced to about 300ml/10½fl oz/1¼ cups. Leave to cool completely.

Transfer the pears to a large serving bowl or individual bowls and strain the cooled syrup over the top. Chill in the refrigerator and serve cold, with Greek yogurt, if you like.

rhubarb and ginger dairy-free fool

200g/7oz/1⅔ cups
  cashew nuts
400g/14oz rhubarb,
  chopped into pieces
2½ tbsp finely chopped
  root ginger
juice and zest of
  ½ orange
100ml/3½fl oz/scant
  ½ cup agave syrup

Usually fruit fools have the reputation of being very indulgent and naughty as they are made with full-fat cream and often custard, too. This is a very healthy version that can fool anyone (sorry I couldn't resist!).

Put the cashews in a bowl and cover with water. Leave to soak for about 2 hours to soften.

Meanwhile, put the rhubarb, ginger and orange juice and zest in a saucepan over a medium-low heat. Cover with a lid and cook for about 10 minutes until the rhubarb has cooked down to a pulp, stirring occasionally. Remove from the heat and leave to cool completely.

When cold, blitz the rhubarb and ginger with the agave syrup in a food processor until it forms a smooth purée.

Drain the softened cashews and put in a food processor with 125ml/4fl oz/½ cup cold water. Blend until completely smooth and the consistency of smooth, light, fluffy whipped cream.

Fold in half of the rhubarb and ginger purée until well combined. Gently fold in the remaining purée, leaving a slightly rippled effect. Spoon into individual glasses or dishes and chill for at least 1 hour before serving.

*WHY NOT TRY...

Making this fool with other fruit purées. The sweeter the fruit, the less agave syrup will be required. My favourites are mango purée with lime zest, or apple and blackberry. If you wanted to make a richer, thicker fruit fool, then you could fold through some soy custard.

MAKES ABOUT 1.2L/
40FL OZ/5 CUPS
preparation time: 10 minutes,
plus freezing

banana, peanut and maple frozen yogurt

3 ripe bananas, peeled
and chopped
200g/7oz/1½ cups
unsalted peanuts
5 tbsp maple syrup, plus
extra to taste
400ml/14fl oz/1⅔ cups
low-fat Greek yogurt
200ml/7fl oz/scant 1 cup
low-fat coconut milk

Frozen yogurt has a much fresher and lighter flavour than ice cream, not to mention a far lower fat content. This recipe provides a brilliant mix of nutrients including protein, vitamin E and fibre from the peanuts, potassium in the bananas and plenty of calcium from the yogurt and milk. Maple syrup is a good way to sweeten up the frozen yogurt as it's a natural sweetener and therefore much better for you than sugar. Try and make sure you use 100% pure maple syrup (in this recipe and all my other recipes), otherwise you could be adding a whole load of artificial additives, sweeteners and preservatives to the mix, which really does defeat the object of being healthy.

Put the bananas in a single layer on a tray lined with cling film/plastic wrap. Put in the freezer for at least 2 hours until frozen solid.

Put the peanuts in a food processor and blitz until they form a really smooth consistency that looks like peanut butter. Be patient with this as it will take a good few minutes to reach the right consistency.

Add the frozen bananas and maple syrup. Blitz well until smooth and creamy.

Mix in the Greek yogurt and coconut milk. Have a taste and add extra maple syrup if you prefer a sweeter flavour.

Transfer to the bowl of an ice-cream machine and churn according to the manufacturer's instructions, or see the tip below on freezing.

Either serve as soon as it is softly frozen, or transfer to a suitable container and freeze until required.

✳ PS... If you don't have an ice-cream machine, pour the mixture into a shallow freezer-proof container or roasting pan. Freeze for about 30 minutes until the edges are frozen. Whisk to break down any ice crystals using a balloon whisk and return to the freezer. Repeat this process until it has frozen. For a super-smooth frozen yogurt, give it a brief blitz in a food processor before serving.

dairy-free vanilla and blueberry cheesecake

For the base:

4 tbsp melted coconut oil, melted, plus extra for greasing

150g/5½oz/1⅓ cups pecan nuts

150g/5½oz/1¼ cups dates, pitted and roughly chopped

100g/3½oz/⅔ cup oatmeal

For the filling:

1 tbsp cornflour/ cornstarch

2 tbsp lemon juice

500g/1lb 2oz firm silken tofu

125ml/4fl oz/½ cup maple syrup

2 eggs, lightly beaten

seeds from 2 vanilla pods/beans

finely grated zest of 1 lemon

For the topping:

200g/7oz/1½ cups blueberries

2 tbsp maple syrup

2 tsp lemon juice

OK, so this isn't a proper cheesecake because it doesn't actually contain any cream cheese at all. That said, it looks and tastes like a baked cheesecake and is fantastically healthy at the same time. The base is a clever mix of oatmeal, dates (to naturally sweeten), coconut oil and pecan nuts, so no overly sweet, shop-bought biscuits here. The creamy filling is made using silken tofu and eggs, and is classically flavoured using vanilla seeds and some lemon for added zest. This is a high-protein, low-fat filling that will go down a treat and even non-tofu fans will be impressed with this dessert (and if you don't tell them they wouldn't even know it is in there). Antioxidant-rich blueberries are a classic baked cheesecake topping that complete this dessert perfectly, but you could use any other seasonal fruit.

Preheat the oven to 160°C/315°F/gas 2–3. Brush a little melted coconut oil around the base and sides of a 20cm/8in cake pan.

Put the pecans in a small roasting pan and toast in the oven for 5 minutes until they become a little darker. Leave to cool slightly, then tip into a food processor. Blitz to a coarse crumb. Add the dates, coconut oil and oatmeal. Briefly blitz until the mixture begins to stick together. Press firmly and evenly into the base of the prepared pan.

To make the filling, mix the cornflour/cornstarch and lemon juice to a smooth paste. Put in a food processor with all the remaining filling ingredients and blitz until completely smooth. Pour over the base and bake for 40 minutes, or until the top is very lightly golden and the middle is just set, but still has a little wobble when you tap the pan. Leave to cool, then chill for about 2 hours.

To make the topping, put the blueberries in a saucepan with the maple syrup and lemon juice. Set over a medium heat and bring to a simmer, stirring occasionally. Cook for about 1 minute until some of the blueberries burst open, making a deep blue juice in the pan. Remove from the heat and leave to cool to room temperature.

Remove the chilled cheesecake from the pan and spoon the blueberries over. Serve cut into wedges.

turkish delight chocolate mousse

75g/2½oz dark/
   bittersweet chocolate
   (70% cocoa solids),
   roughly chopped
3 egg whites
3 tbsp agave syrup
I ripe small to medium
   avocado, peeled and
   pitted
¼ tsp rosewater, plus
   extra to taste

To decorate:
I tbsp roughly chopped
   pistachio nuts
a pinch of dried edible
   rose petals (optional)

This rose-scented chocolate mousse is rich and creamy, yet not as bad for you in comparison to a standard chocolate mousse. Instead of cream, the mousse is made with avocados, which give a thick creamy texture and also make this dessert dairy-free, much lower in saturated fat and loaded with antioxidants and omegas. As for the chocolate – well, providing you use a high cocoa-solid chocolate (such as 70%) you will be consuming less sugar and even more antioxidants, iron and magnesium than other types of chocolate. In my book that makes this delicious dessert completely guilt-free!

Melt the chocolate either in a heatproof bowl set over a pan of gently simmering water, making sure the bottom of the bowl does not touch the water. Alternatively, gently melt on a low heat in the microwave. Stir occasionally until the chocolate has melted. Leave to cool to room temperature.

In a separate bowl, whisk the egg whites until they form soft peaks. Add the agave syrup and continue whisking until they form firm peaks.

Blend the avocado and rosewater with a hand-held/immersion blender until completely smooth, then mix into the chocolate. If the avocado isn't smooth enough, you can press it through a sieve/fine mesh strainer using a spatula to remove any lumps. Mix in one spoonful of the egg whites to loosen the mixture, then gently fold in the rest.

Spoon the mousse into glasses or dishes. Chill for about 2 hours, then scatter with the chopped pistachios and rose petals, if using, and serve.

PS... If you want to ring the changes and try something other than rosewater to flavour the chocolate mousse, you could add the zest of I orange, I teaspoon ground cinnamon, a few drops of coconut extract or a pinch of ground cardamom seeds.

blackberry and honey soufflés

300g/10½oz/2¼ cups
  blackberries, plus extra
  to serve
1 ripe banana, peeled and
  mashed
a little melted coconut
  oil, for brushing
3 tbsp chopped nuts,
  ground almonds or
  grated chocolate
6 tbsp honey
4 egg whites
Greek yogurt, to serve
  (optional)

Generally soufflés are not as bad for you as people think. They are high in protein from the eggs and actually a lovely light dessert to end a meal. Their downfall, though, is that they can contain quite a lot of sugar. So, rather than outing soufflés on my naughty list, I've had a play around and swapped the sugar with ripened bananas (the riper they are the sweeter they become) and honey. The honey is boiled to reduce in quantity, really intensifying its flavour and sweetness. The result is stunning and the soufflés are also pretty easy to make, which busts another soufflé myth.

Preheat the oven to 200°C/400°F/gas 6 and place a baking sheet in the oven to heat up.

Put the blackberries in a saucepan with 2 tablespoons water. Cover with a lid and cook over a low heat for about 10 minutes, or until they have softened and broken down. Add the banana and then blitz to a smooth purée with a hand-held/immersion blender.

Brush 6 ramekins with a little oil. Coat the inside of each ramekin evenly with the chopped nuts by tipping and rolling them around to stick to the sides and bases of the ramekins.

Put the honey in a small saucepan and bring to the boil. Continue to boil for 1–2 minutes until it becomes deep golden.

Meanwhile, whisk the egg whites until they form firm peaks. Gradually pour in the hot honey, continuing to whisk, until you have a firm and slightly glossy consistency. Mix in one-third of the blackberry and banana purée, then gently fold in the rest with a metal spoon until combined.

Spoon evenly into the prepared ramekin dishes and level the tops with a palette knife/metal spatula. Put the ramekins on the preheated baking sheet and bake for 10–12 minutes until well risen and lightly golden.

Carefully transfer the soufflés to serving plates and serve immediately with extra blackberries and dollops of Greek yogurt, if you like.

SERVES 8

preparation time: 20 minutes,
plus 30 minutes chilling
cooking time: 50–65 minutes

plum and almond tart

450g/1lb ripe juicy plums
2–4 tbsp honey or agave
    syrup, plus extra for
    drizzling
40g/1½oz/½ cup toasted
    flaked/sliced almonds

For the pastry:
75g/2½oz/¾ cup ground
    almonds
75g/2½oz/heaped ½ cup
    blanched hazelnuts
4 tbsp rolled oats
75g/2½oz/heaped ⅓ cup
    pitted dates
3 tbsp melted coconut oil
    or olive oil
freshly grated nutmeg
sea salt

This pastry base is a handy recipe for many sweet desserts as it's far lower in saturated fat than rich buttery, traditional pastry and is bursting with vitamins and minerals from the nuts and dates. I like to use it to make pumpkin pie or as an alternative biscuit base for banoffee pie.

To make the 'pastry', put the ground almonds, hazelnuts and oats in a food processor and blitz to a fine crumb. Add the dates, coconut oil, a pinch of salt and a really generous grating of nutmeg. Blitz well to a thick doughy consistency.

Press the dough into a 20cm/8in loose-bottomed tart pan, pushing into the edges and up the sides to evenly line the inside of the pan. Chill for about 30 minutes.

Preheat the oven to 180°C/350°F/gas 4.

Scrunch up a large piece of baking parchment and put in the tart, making sure the edges of the pastry are loosely covered with the paper. Cover the base with baking beans or rice and bake for 15 minutes. Remove the baking parchment and baking beans and cook for a further 5 minutes until the pastry is firm and lightly golden.

Reduce the oven temperature to 160°C/315°F/gas 2–3. Cut the plums in half and remove the pits, then cut each half into 2 or 3 wedges, depending on their size.

Arrange the plums inside the tart, working from the outside in, packing the fruit into the case/shell. Drizzle with honey or agave syrup. If the plums are quite tart or not very juicy, you may need a little more.

Bake for 30–45 minutes until the plums are soft and starting to take on golden tinges. Leave to cool in the pan for 10 minutes or so before removing carefully. Drizzle over extra honey or agave for a glossy finish, and scatter with flaked/sliced almonds before serving warm or at room temperature.

crunchy baked peach melba crumble

4 ripe but firm large
   peaches or nectarines,
   halved and pitted
150g/5½oz/heaped 1 cup
   raspberries
2 tbsp melted coconut oil
2 tbsp honey
50g/1¾oz/½ cup rolled
   oats
2 tbsp ground almonds
2 tbsp flaked/sliced
   almonds
2 tbsp pumpkin seeds
zest of ½ orange
½ tsp ground cinnamon

Traditionally, crumble toppings are made by rubbing butter into flour and sugar with a few optional extras added along the way for flavour and crunch. To give this a healthier twist, I use coconut oil to mix into the oats mixture and sweeten it with honey. The addition of flaked/sliced almonds and pumpkin seeds provides added loveliness and the flavoursome orange and cinnamon give the topping that little extra something – it's delicious. You can make this all year round, changing the fruits depending on the season. Trade the peaches and raspberries for strawberries, plums, blackberries, poached rhubarb or cooked pears and apple, and add a little honey to the fruits depending on their acidity.

Preheat the oven to 180°C/350°F/gas 4. Place the peaches, cut side up, in a shallow baking dish. Scatter the raspberries into the dish around the peaches.

Combine the oil, honey, oats, ground and flaked/sliced almonds, pumpkin seeds, orange zest and cinnamon, mixing well to make sure everything is coated in the oil and honey.

Scatter the crumble topping over the top of the peaches and bake in the oven for 10–15 minutes until the peaches are soft and juicy and the crumble is golden and crunchy.

PS... You could increase the quantity of the crumble
mix and cook it in a single layer on a baking sheet for
10–15 minutes until golden and crunchy. Leave to cool
and use as a breakfast topping scattered over yogurt
or fruit. Store any unused crumble in an airtight
container for up to 1 week.

flourless red velvet chocolate torte

olive oil, for greasing

200g/7oz dark/
bittersweet chocolate
(70% cocoa solids),
broken into small
pieces

300g/10½oz raw
beetroot/beets, washed
and roughly chopped

6 eggs, separated

100g/3½oz/½ cup soft
brown sugar

2 tsp vanilla extract

75g/2½oz/¾ cup ground
almonds

125g/4½oz/½ cup Greek
yogurt

1 tbsp cocoa powder or
icing/confectioners'
sugar, for dusting

Far healthier than your average chocolate torte, this has the addition of health-boosting beetroot and a lower fat content due to the absence of butter. It's chocolatey and rich in flavour, light in texture and such a beautiful colour. You'd never know the beetroot was in there if it wasn't for the colour it provides. Serve as a dinner party dessert and enjoy the leftovers (if there are any) over the next few days with a cup of tea – how delightful.

Preheat the oven to 180°C/350°F/gas 4. Grease a 20cm/8in round loose-bottomed or springform cake pan with a little oil.

Melt the chocolate in a small heatproof bowl set over a pan of gently simmering water, making sure the bottom of the bowl does not touch the water. Alternatively, gently melt on a low heat in the microwave. Stir occasionally until the chocolate has melted.

Put the beetroot/beets in a food processor, add 80ml/2½fl oz/⅓ cup water and blitz to a smooth purée, scraping down the sides when necessary.

Using an electric mixer, beat the egg yolks with the sugar until thick and creamy. Stir in the beetroot/beet purée, melted chocolate, vanilla extract, ground almonds and Greek yogurt until completely mixed.

In a separate bowl, whisk the egg whites until thick and they hold a firm peak when the whisk is lifted. Gently fold into the chocolate mixture until all of the egg white is combined. Transfer to the prepared pan and bake for 35 minutes until the middle is just firm. To check, insert a skewer into the middle of the torte and if it comes out clean it is cooked. If not, continue to cook for a further 5 minutes. Turn off the heat and leave the torte in the oven for 10 minutes before removing.

Leave the torte to cool in the pan for about 30 minutes before serving warm, or leave to cool to room temperature.

Dust with cocoa powder and serve cut into wedges.

Any torte not eaten on the day of baking can be stored in the refrigerator for up to 3 days.

chia seed flapjacks

MAKES 15

preparation time: 10 minutes
cooking time: 40 minutes

6 tbsp coconut oil, plus
   extra for greasing
175g/6oz/1¾ cups rolled
   oats
100g/3½oz/scant 1 cup
   pecan nuts, roughly
   chopped
50g/1¾oz/⅔ cup
   pumpkin or sunflower
   seeds
50g/1¾oz/⅓ cup chia
   seeds
40g/1½oz/1 cup flaked
   coconut
75g/2½oz/½ cup dried
   cherries, cranberries
   or blueberries
100g/3½oz/⅔ cup
   chopped dried figs
   or pitted dates
½ tsp vanilla extract
115g/4oz/generous ⅓ cup
   honey
3 tbsp soft brown sugar

If you've not already done so, have a read about how great chia seeds are (see page 210). You'd be foolish not to give these 'power' flapjacks a go – the energy you get from them will keep you going for ages, meaning you won't snack on whatever is lying around later on in the day.

Preheat the oven to 180°C/350°F/gas 4. Grease a 20 x 30cm/8 x 12in cake pan with oil and line the base with baking parchment.

Put the oats, pecans and pumpkin seeds in a baking pan and toast in the oven for 10 minutes, stirring occasionally, until lightly golden. Tip into a bowl and mix with the chia seeds, coconut flakes, dried fruit and vanilla extract.

In a small pan, heat together the coconut oil, honey and sugar, stirring until the sugar has dissolved and the mixture starts to boil. Simmer for 2 minutes, then pour over the oat mixture. Mix well, then tip into the prepared pan. Press into the edges with the back of a spoon and bake for 25–30 minutes until lightly golden on top.

Leave in the pan until completely cool, then turn out and cut into squares.

The flapjacks will keep in an airtight container for up to 2 weeks.

incredible chia

If you're not yet familiar with chia seeds, then it's time for you to get to know these tiny little balls of goodness because they are among the healthiest foods on the planet. They are the size of poppyseeds and come in either black/ grey or white. They can be easily found in health food shops (numerous supermarkets sell them, too), and their popularity is increasing all the time.

origins

Chia seeds originate from a flowering plant in the mint family called *Salvia hispanica* that is native to Mexico and Guatemala, and they are said to have been the food of choice of the Aztecs and Mayans due to their ability to provide sustainable energy. In fact, 'chia' is the ancient Mayan word for 'strength', and a single tablespoon would keep them going for 24 hours!

nutrition

Don't be fooled by their size – these tiny seeds pack a powerful, nutritional punch. As well as providing energy, they are ridiculously high in fibre, omega-3 fats, protein and antioxidants. They are low in calories, classed as a 'whole grain' and naturally gluten free. The recommended daily serving is only 1 tablespoon (15g/½oz), which is incredibly easy to include in your daily diet.

uses of chia

The seeds taste pretty bland alone, so you should add them to other things, such as cereals, yogurt, salads and veggie or rice dishes. Stir them into soups, porridge and stews, blend them into smoothies or add to your baking, such as bread, cakes and muffins. The thing about chia seeds that amazes me the most is that they absorb so much liquid (12 times their weight) and can therefore be used to thicken sauces, make puddings and used as a substitute for eggs in pretty much most recipes.

When mixed with liquid, the seeds plump up, forming a gel layer around each seed, which then acts as a binder in the same way eggs do.

To create an egg substitute, simply mix 1 tablespoon chia seeds with 3 tablespoons water or other liquid such as milk or juice. Leave to soak for about 5–10 minutes until you have a gloopy gel equivalent to one whole beaten egg. Each 1 tablespoon of chia seed is equivalent to one egg, so increase quantities of chia seed and liquid according to your recipe.

It's worth pointing out that once made, chia seeds still retain a slightly crunchy texture when in gel form. For many recipes this is just fine, such as in baking, but you can grind the seeds in a blender or coffee grinder before mixing with liquid for a smoother end result. This is particularly useful when making puddings or sauces.

recipe inspiration

As well as my Chia Seed Flapjacks on page 208, there are many other exciting ways to use them. Experiment yourself, or try one of these recipes.

lemon chia caesar salad dressing

This is great to use as a salad dressing with crunchy Cos lettuce, crispy bread croutons and some shavings of Parmesan cheese. It also works really well as a dip for crudités or tossed into cooked new potatoes for a very tasty potato salad.

Put 3 tablespoons lemon juice, 2 tablespoons chia seeds, 3 tablespoons avocado or extra virgin olive oil, 1 anchovy fillet, 1 small peeled garlic clove, 1 teaspoon Dijon mustard and 1 teaspoon honey in a blender and blitz until smooth. Season to taste with salt and pepper. Serves 4.

spicy crusted sweet potato wedges

Add some additional goodness and crunch to baked potato wedges.

Mix together 2 tablespoons chia seeds with ½ teaspoon smoked paprika, a pinch of chilli powder, 1 teaspoon ground coriander, 2 tablespoons olive or hempseed oil and a good pinch of salt. Toss together with 2 sweet potatoes cut into fairly slim wedges. Lay on a baking sheet and bake in a preheated oven set to 200°C/400°F/gas 6 for about 20–30 minutes, turning occasionally, until tender and turning golden. Serves 2.

chocolate chia pancakes

These are such a tasty treat for breakfast. I first made these when I promised the family pancakes for breakfast and then realized we were out of eggs. Cue chia seeds and I was saved, phew! So whether you are out of eggs, need to avoid eggs in your diet or simply want to try something different, these chia pancakes are well worth a go.

Put 2 tablespoons chia seeds and 6 tablespoons milk into a large bowl and leave for 10 minutes to thicken. Sift in 200g/7oz/1½ cups plain/ all-purpose flour, 3 tablespoons cocoa powder and 1 tablespoon baking powder. Then add 2 tablespoons golden caster/raw cane sugar, 2 tablespoons melted coconut oil and 300ml/10½ fl oz/1¼ cups milk. Whisk well until combined. Heat a pancake pan over a medium-low heat and brush with a little more coconut oil. Drop large tablespoonfuls of the batter into the pan, cooking 3–4 at a time, and cook for 2–3 minutes until small bubbles appear on the surface of the pancakes. Turn over and cook for a further 2–3 minutes. Remove from the pan and continue with the remaining batter – it should make about 16. These fluffy, chocolatey pancakes are delicious served with maple or agave syrup, sliced bananas, chopped toasted hazelnuts and a dollop of Greek yogurt.

raspberry and vanilla chia jam

This is a brilliant quick version of jam that doesn't require cooking or lots of sugar. Serve this in the same way as traditional jam or spoon onto puddings.

Soak 2 tablespoons chia seeds in 3 tablespoons water and leave for 10 minutes. Put in a blender or food processor with 175g/6oz/1¼ cups fresh or defrosted raspberries, ½ teaspoon vanilla bean paste and 3 tablespoons honey, agave syrup or golden caster/raw cane sugar and blitz to combine, then transfer to a clean jar. Leave to stand for 10 minutes, then enjoy straight away or store in the refrigerator and use within 1 week. Makes about 200ml/7fl oz/scant 1 cup.

sugar-free pear, pecan and spelt cookies

1 ripe pear, peeled

100g/3½oz/¾ cup spelt
   flour

50g/1¾oz/½ cup rolled
   oats

½ tsp baking powder

½ tsp ground ginger

50g/1¾oz/½ cup pecan
   nuts, roughly chopped

60ml/2fl oz/¼ cup
   maple syrup

60ml/2fl oz/¼ cup
   rapeseed/canola or
   coconut oil

These are a perfect pick-me-up treat when you crave something sweet without the ingredient of guilt. They're wonderfully quick and easy to make – though do be warned, they are very moreish. I like to use spelt flour in these cookies as it has a slightly nuttier flavour than wheat flour, it's higher in protein, lower in gluten and a great source of slow-release energy. If you prefer, standard wheat flour can be used instead of the spelt flour.

Preheat the oven to 180°C/350°F/gas 4. Line two baking sheets with baking parchment.

Grate the pear into a bowl so you catch any juices; discard the core.

Add all of the remaining ingredients and mix until well combined. Spoon 12 dollops of the cookie mixture onto the prepared baking sheets and flatten lightly with the back of the spoon. Bake for 18–20 minutes until golden.

Remove from the oven and leave to cool for about 10 minutes before removing from the sheet and leaving to cool completely on a wire/cooling rack.

The cookies will keep in an airtight container for up to 1 week.

*WHY NOT TRY...

Swapping the pear and pecans with apple and walnuts.

Grated orange zest can also be added for a fruitier flavour.

chocolate pumpkin brownies

olive oil, for greasing

For the pumpkin mix:
175g/6oz peeled and
    deseeded raw pumpkin
    or squash, cut into
    small pieces
75g/2½oz/⅓ cup low-fat
    cream cheese
2 tbsp maple syrup
2 egg yolks
1 tsp ground cinnamon

For the chocolate mix:
100g/3¾oz/¾ cup plain/
    all-purpose flour
1 tsp baking powder
250g/9oz/1 cup Greek
    yogurt
2 egg whites
2 tsp vanilla extract
a pinch of salt
125ml/4fl oz/½ cup
    maple syrup
55g/2oz/½ cup cocoa
    powder
55g/2oz/½ cup pecan
    nuts, roughly chopped
    (optional)

There are many healthy alternative recipes for chocolate brownies, which is a blessing for chocoholics out there wanting to ease their consciences. These dense, fudgy brownies are swirled with a vitamin-rich pumpkin purée and are a lot lower in fat than traditional brownies, which usually contain a lot of butter. And as for sweetness, I use maple syrup, the natural sweetness of pumpkin and some ground cinnamon, which seems to magically enhance the sweetness of the pumpkin even further. I'm not going to pretend these are comparable to traditional brownies, but they are a very moreish, low-fat, sugar-free, nutrient-rich alternative.

Steam the pumpkin in a steamer set over a pan of simmering water for about 10 minutes until completely tender. Mash or blend to a smooth purée and leave to cool slightly.

Preheat the oven to 180°C/350°F/gas 4. Brush a 20cm/8in square cake pan with a little oil and line the base with baking parchment.

For the chocolate mix, simply put all of the ingredients in a food processor and blend until a smooth batter forms. Pour into the prepared cake pan.

Mix the remaining pumpkin mix ingredients into the pumpkin purée until smooth.

Using a tablespoon, drop dollops of the pumpkin purée all over the top of the chocolate mixture. Using a fork, loosely swirl the pumpkin into the chocolate mixture, taking care not to overmix. Bake for about 20–25 minutes until the top is set and the brownie begins to come away from the sides of the pan. Leave to cool in the pan before removing and cutting into squares.

The brownies will keep in the refrigerator for up to 3 days.

preparation time: 15 minutes,
plus cooling

cooking time: about 1 hour

400g/14oz peeled sweet
  potatoes, cut into
  chunks
185ml/6fl oz/¾ cup
  olive oil, plus extra for
  greasing
200g/7oz/2 cups ground
  almonds
4 eggs, lightly beaten
100g/3½oz/½ cup soft
  light brown sugar
2 tbsp baking powder
1 tsp vanilla extract
finely grated zest of
  1 lemon
finely grated zest of
  2 oranges

st clement's sweet potato cake

Sweet potatoes are packed with beta-carotene, which gives them their bright orange colour and is very good for your eyesight and skin, protecting collagen from damage, reducing inflammation and redness and generally keeping you looking young. So, make this and you might actually take a few years off yourself.

Cook the sweet potatoes in a steamer set over boiling water for 15–20 minutes until tender. Press through a potato ricer or mash well. Leave to cool.

Preheat the oven to 180°C/350°F/gas 4. Lightly oil a deep 20cm/8in round cake pan and line the base with baking parchment.

Put the cooled potatoes into a large bowl and add the ground almonds, olive oil, eggs, sugar, baking powder, vanilla and orange and lemon zest. Mix well.

Spoon the batter into the cake pan, smooth over the surface and bake for 45–50 minutes until just firm and a skewer inserted into the middle of the cake comes out clean. Leave to cool in the pan for 15 minutes before turning out onto a wire/cooling rack to cool completely.

The cake will keep in an airtight container for up to 5 days.

*WHY NOT TRY...

Adding a teaspoon of finely chopped rosemary
to the cake batter. It adds a wonderful flavour and
has a lovely aromatic scent when baking.

irresistible carrot cake with coconut-lime frosting

preparation time: 30 minutes,
plus overnight chilling
and cooling
cooking time: 45 minutes

200ml/7fl oz/scant 1 cup
   rapeseed/canola oil,
   plus extra for greasing
1 large ripe banana,
   peeled and mashed
   to a purée
125ml/4fl oz/½ cup
   maple syrup
3 eggs, lightly beaten
225g/8oz/1¾ cups
   wholegrain spelt flour
1 tbsp baking powder
1½ tsp bicarbonate of
   soda/baking soda
1½ tsp ground cinnamon
½ tsp ground allspice
½ tsp ground ginger
275g/9¾oz/2 cups finely
   grated carrots
115g/4oz/heaped ¾ cup
   sultanas/golden raisins
40g/1½oz/½ cup
   desiccated/dried
   shredded coconut

For the frosting:
400ml/14fl oz can
   full-fat coconut milk,
   chilled overnight
150g/5½oz/⅔ cup cream
   cheese
finely grated zest of
   2 limes
4 tbsp maple syrup

This is a favourite recipe of mine that I've tweaked in various ways to make it a little healthier. Instead of using sugar, I've swapped it for naturally sweet mashed banana and pure maple syrup and it's made with omega-rich rapeseed/canola oil (super-healthy coconut oil could be used if you wish). As an alternative to flour, I've used wholegrain spelt flour, which provides plenty of fibre and a lower wheat content than traditional wheat flour. When it comes to the topping, forget buttery, sugary frostings — the cloud-like frosting is made by whisking the top part of a chilled can of coconut milk with cream cheese, maple syrup and lime. You'll be amazed at the result you get. This is a delicious cake that can be served any time of the day, for any occasion whether mid-morning, afternoon tea, dinner party dessert or even as a celebration cake.

Preheat the oven to 160°C/350°F/gas 4. Lightly brush a deep 20cm/8in round cake pan with a little oil and line the base with baking parchment.

In a large bowl, mix together the oil, mashed banana, maple syrup and eggs until totally combined. Mix in all of the remaining cake ingredients and spoon into the prepared pan. Bake for 40–45 minutes until nicely risen and firm but springy when lightly pressed. You can insert a skewer into the middle of the cake if you are not sure, and if it comes out clean, it is cooked. Leave the cake to cool in the pan for 10 minutes before turning out onto a wire/cooling rack to cool completely.

To make the frosting, scoop the thick white layer of chilled coconut milk into a mixing bowl (leaving the liquid behind) and whisk with a hand-held electric mixer until it becomes thick and creamy, like whipped cream. Add the cream cheese, lime zest and maple syrup and whisk to combine. Chill for about 20 minutes.

When the cake is cool, spread the frosting over the top and serve cut into wedges. The cake will keep in the refrigerator for up to 3 days.

MAKES 1 LOAF
preparation time: 20 minutes
cooking time: 50 minutes

courgette, pistachio and orange loaf cake

125ml/4fl oz/½ cup
  olive oil, plus extra for
  greasing
2 eggs
100g/3½oz/½ cup soft
  brown sugar
2 tsp vanilla extract
350g/12oz/4 cups
  coarsely grated
  courgette/zucchini
finely grated zest of
  1 orange
300g/10½oz/2¼ cups
  wholegrain spelt or
  wholemeal/whole-wheat
  flour
75g/2½oz/½ cup shelled
  pistachio nuts, roughly
  chopped
1 tsp baking powder
1 tsp ground cinnamon

For the orange glaze (optional):
60g/2¼oz/½ cup icing/
  confectioners' sugar,
  sifted
juice and zest of about
  ½ orange
1 tbsp roughly chopped
  pistachio nuts

This pretty loaf cake is packed with flavour and uses courgette/zucchini as its secret ingredient, making it slightly more healthy for you. I like to use spelt or wholemeal/whole-wheat flour for extra goodness, too. The orange glaze really lifts this cake to another level of tastiness.

Preheat the oven to 180°C/350°F/gas 4. Oil a 1kg/2lb 4oz loaf pan and line the base with baking parchment.

Lightly beat together the eggs, olive oil, sugar and vanilla extract. Stir in the grated courgette/zucchini and orange zest.

In a separate bowl, combine the flour, pistachio nuts, baking powder and cinnamon. Pour in the egg mixture and mix everything together well.

Pour the batter into the prepared pan and smooth the surface with the back of a spoon. Bake for 45–50 minutes, or until a skewer comes out clean when inserted in the middle of the loaf. If the cake starts to brown too much, cover the top with foil. Leave to cool in the pan for 10 minutes before turning out onto a wire/cooling rack to cool completely.

To make the orange glaze, if using, put the icing/confectioners' sugar in a bowl with the orange zest and gradually mix in enough orange juice to form a runny icing. Pour over the cake, allowing it to drip down the sides, then scatter over the pistachios.

The cake will keep in an airtight container for up to 1 week.

index

A

almonds: plum and almond tart 204

apples: apple, cranberry and walnut gluten-free loaf 30

    apple purée 27

    carrot, ginger and apple soup 80

artichokes: spelt and hemp pizzas 176

Asian coleslaw 82

asparagus: smoked salmon, samphire and asparagus salad 64

avocados: avocado, carrot and cucumber temaki 98

    poached eggs, tahini and pan-fried avocado 36

    roast mushrooms and avocado on rye 35

    sea bass ceviche with papaya and avocado 72

    smoked trout and beetroot frittata with avocado salsa 68

B

bananas: banana and date muffins 28

    banana and spelt pancakes with blueberry compôte 34

    banana, matcha and honey smoothie 17

    banana, peanut and maple frozen yogurt 197

barley: pearl barley and mushroom risotto with goats' cheese 182

    soft-boiled egg and barley salad 94

    winter vegetable broth with zesty parsley dressing 81

beans: Cajun chicken with beans and greens salad 104

    sprouting 58–9

    super shepherd's pie 128

beef: beef and quinoa meatballs 122

    beef carpaccio with rocket and alfalfa salad 56

    beef, squash and mango pilau 126

    stir-fried chilli beef and rice noodles 119

    Vietnamese beef skewers with pickled carrot salad 60

beetroot: beetroot gnocchi with nutty watercress pesto 170

    flourless red velvet chocolate torte 206

    mackerel and quinoa salad with wasabi dressing 73

    pan-fried mackerel with wheat berry salad 152

    smoked trout and beetroot frittata with avocado salsa 68

berries: apple, cranberry and walnut gluten-free loaf 30

    blackberry and goji smoothie 16

    blackberry and honey soufflés 202

    crunchy baked peach melba crumble 205

    dairy-free vanilla and blueberry cheesecake 198

    ginger berry muffins 27

    raspberry and vanilla chia jam 211

    raspberry yogurt crunch pots 22

    Swedish pork meatballs with goji berry sauce 54

    warm goats' cheese, blueberry and walnut salad 91

brill: tray-baked brill and Puy lentils with salsa verde 142

broccoli: Thai salmon skewers with edamame quinoa 144

brownies, chocolate pumpkin 214

buckwheat and coconut crêpes with baked figs 32

bulgur wheat pilaf with roast figs, kale and 164

burgers, salmon with pickled radish and wasabi mayo 148

C

cakes: apple, cranberry and walnut gluten-free loaf 30

    banana and date muffins 28

    chocolate pumpkin brownies 214

    courgette, pistachio and orange loaf cake 218

    ginger berry muffins 27

    irresistible carrot cake with coconut-lime frosting 216

    St Clement's sweet potato cake 215

carpaccio, beef with rocket and alfalfa salad 56

carrots: avocado, carrot and cucumber temaki 98

    carrot, ginger and apple soup 80

    carrot salad 162

    irresistible carrot cake with coconut-lime frosting 216

    lamb and chickpea koftas with sesame carrot mash 132

    roast carrot and feta salad with tahini dressing 86

    Vietnamese beef skewers with pickled carrot salad 60

cashews: strawberries with vanilla cashew cream 190

casseroles see stews and casseroles

cauliflower: cauliflower couscous 90, 114

    cauliflower curry with fresh mango pickle 162

    cauliflower soup 172

    cauliflower steaks with capers, chard and lentils 172

celery: ginger chicken with cucumber and celery slaw 52

ceviche, sea bass with papaya and avocado 72

chard: braised venison sausages with Puy lentils and chard 134

    cauliflower steaks with capers, chard and lentils 172

cheese: feta, pea and mint quinoa salad 180

    herby chickpea tabbouleh with oven-dried tomatoes 92

    pearl barley and mushroom risotto with goats' cheese 182

    roast carrot and feta salad with tahini dressing 86

    warm goats' cheese, blueberry and walnut salad 91

cheesecake, dairy-free vanilla and blueberry 198

NOURISH

EAT WELL, LIVE WELL

Here at Nourish we're all about wellbeing through food and drink – irresistible dishes with a serious good-for-you factor.
If you want to eat and drink delicious things that set you up for the day, suit any special diets, keep you healthy and make
the most of the ingredients you have, we've got some great ideas to share with you. Come over to our blog for wholesome
recipes and fresh inspiration – **nourishbooks.com.**